NEW STARS FOR A NEW ERA

A CONSCIOUSNESS WORKBOOK FOR OUR 10 NEW PLANETS

A Dwarf Planet University Publication

Copyright © Alan Clay 2024

Artmedia
72 / 26 Antill St
Dickson ACT 2602
Australia

www.dwarfplanet.university
alan@artmedia.com.au

New Stars for a New Era

ISBN: 978-0-6458033-2-7

Planet images by astrologer, Karen La Puma
Author of the series *A Toolkit for Awakening*
www.karenlapuma.com

Edited by Melissa Billington and Armand Diaz

Design by Steve Williams, RedInc® & Alan Clay

A big thank you to my assistant Melissa Billington and to the students at the Dwarf Planet University whose collective research has enabled this book.

All Rights Reserved.

This work is copyright. Except for the purposes of fair reviewing, no part of this publication may be reproduced or transmitted in any form or by any means, without permission in writing from the publisher. The moral right of the author has been asserted.

NEW STARS
FOR A
NEW ERA

**A CONSCIOUSNESS WORKBOOK FOR OUR
10 NEW PLANETS**

Alan Clay

Contents

We Live in a Dynamic System ... 1
New Stars for a New Era ... 5
Consciousness Workbook ... 17
Ixion ... 21
    Ixion Consciousness Challenges ... 25
    Ixion in the Houses ... 27
Orcus ... 47
    Orcus Consciousness Challenges ... 50
    Orcus in the Houses ... 53
Salacia ... 73
    Salacia Consciousness Challenges ... 76
    Salacia in the Houses ... 78
Varuna ... 97
    Varuna Consciousness Challenges ... 100
    Varuna in the Houses ... 103
Haumea ... 121
    Haumea Consciousness Challenges ... 125
    Haumea in the Houses ... 127

Quaoar	**145**
Quaoar Consciousness Challenges	147
Quaoar in the Houses	150
Makemake	**169**
Makemake Consciousness Challenges	174
Makemake in the Houses	176
Gonggong	**195**
Gonggong Consciousness Challenges	199
Gonggong in the Houses	202
Eris	**223**
Eris Consciousness Challenges	227
Eris in the Houses	229
Sedna	**249**
Sedna Consciousness Challenges	253
Sedna in the Houses	256
Appendix 1: **Discover Your Dwarf Planets**	295
Appendix 2: **Astrology Basics**	297
Appendix 3: **Dwarf Planets as Higher Octaves**	302
Appendix 4: **Dwarf Planet University**	306
What Students Say	307
Appendix 5: **Meet the Writer**	310

We Live in a Dynamic System

In the scientific worldview of contemporary Western culture, we tend to think that the stars can't really affect us, and that astrology is something akin to magic or a belief system. This assumes we live in a stable world and the planets are merely bits of rock flying around us in space.

The truth is that we live in a dynamic system, and we are influenced by the rhythms of that system. We're on a spinning planet revolving around the Sun, along with all the other planets of our solar system, thanks to the gravitational forces and dynamics of those planets. And meanwhile the whole solar system is travelling at an enormous speed away from the center of the universe, because everything in the universe is moving out from a central point.

Let's look at the Sun. Most people on the planet sleep when it is dark and are active during the day, so our daily rhythm is guided by the rotation of Earth in relation to the big flaming star at the heart of our solar system. We measure a year by the Earth's rotation around the Sun and we see the flow of the year in the seasons, which are created by the angle of the Earth to the Sun. The Sun is so intrinsic to being alive that we don't even think of its effect on us.

Let's look at the Moon. Do you live near the coast? Have you noticed the tides? The gravitational pull of the Moon causes the rise and fall of large bodies of water on the surface of our planet. Our bodies are 90% water, and the Moon's effect on our bodies is clearly evident in the alignment of menstrual cycles with the Moon's monthly cycle.

 Now let's circle back to explode the misconception that astrology is something akin to magic. Magic is when something happens which cannot be rationally explained, and those are wonderful moments that suggests the deep connection of everything in the universe. Astrology does produce such moments, but that is not what we're talking about here.

Nor is astrology a belief system. Astrology is like gravity; you don't need to believe in it for it to have an effect on your life. Astrology is a social science, recording the psychology and behavior of people over the eons, as referenced to the dynamic system in which we live: and that is the only way we measure and record anything. A year is one cycle around the Sun, a day is one revolution of the Earth.

So, over the eons astrologers noticed that we generally sleep at night and go to work during the day. We go out and party on the full moon and stay home and plant gardens on the new moon. That we struggle to make decisions when Mercury, the planet of ideas, seems to be going backwards in the sky. And when Saturn, the planet of responsibility, returns to his birth position when we're about age 29, we all go through a 'What am I doing with my life?' reality check.

The astute reader might then wonder how we get the meanings for the new planets when we don't have the thousands of years of data. The answer is twofold. Firstly, we've noticed that the myth behind the planet's name, and the physical and orbital characteristics of the planet, correlate to its meaning in the dynamic of our lives. So, for the new planets, we can reverse engineer that process to find their meaning from the mythological and physical characteristics.

Secondly, when we apply it to the charts of our lives, we find we do actually have the data. All the planets have been acting in our lives throughout our evolution as a species, we have just been unconscious of the outer celestial bodies, as I will explain in the next chapter. But now that we can see them in the sky, we can see their effect in the events in our lives, and also in the events in peoples' lives throughout history.

New Stars for a New Era

Many astrologers believe that new planets are discovered when we are ready to incorporate the new consciousness represented by that planet into our existing consciousness. We've noticed this with the discovery of Uranus, Neptune, and Pluto over the last two hundred years. Now, with the discovery of ten more outer planets, we're entering a period of rapid consciousness development.

Our personal consciousness develops within the collective consciousness around us, and we see this mapped out in the personal planets in our chart. These are the planets out to Saturn that are visible to the naked eye, and they address facets of our personality that are important in living day to day.

When we are at inner planet consciousness, everything that is important is our feelings, our ideas and values, our agency and the luck and material rewards that these bring us. *"You can't take it with you, right?"* And at this level we tend not to be conscious of the action of the outer planets in our lives.

The inner planets represent aspects of personality, and the outer planets represent aspects of consciousness. So, as each new outer planet is discovered, it represents a new aspect of consciousness that is becoming available to us. Over the last 200 years, we've discovered three new planets. The discovery of Uranus brought us intuitive consciousness, the discovery of Neptune, spiritual consciousness, and the discovery of Pluto, psychological consciousness.

Then, since the turn of the 21st century, we've discovered another ten planets. The discovery of so many new outer planets at one time represents a feast of new consciousness that is now available to us. The enlightenment that until now was only available to select gurus and priests after years of devout work, is now open to everyone.

Because these outer planets talk of consciousness, how they manifest in our lives depends on our own current level of consciousness. Most people on the planet experience the outer planets as unconscious influences. At this level, these esoteric new energies are only perceived when they barge into our lives in a confrontational way, because we haven't been sensitive and adaptable in the lead up.

As we develop spiritually and we consciously on-board these new energies, they become guides into new territory, offering us special skills or challenges, depending on the aspects in our chart. At this level, rather than unconscious influences, the outer planets become like a new super-consciousness.

Let's look briefly at each of the planets beyond Saturn to put them in context.

As we embark on the spiritual path to make a larger sense out of the experiences of our personal lives, we start activating our Uranian and Neptunian energies and bring them into our consciousness. As we do, we begin to realize that the 'you can't take it with you" approach of the inner planets is actually a delusion.

Uranus brings intuitive flashes into our personal planet consciousness and begins to connect us with the collective consciousness, by breaking through our Saturnian defenses to allow new impulses and connections. So, the discovery of Uranus enabled consciousness growth in our lives. We can look at Uranus as the higher octave of Mercury because he takes Mercury's ideas, communications, and curiosity, and networks them at a higher spiritual level.

Neptune tunes us into the bigger picture and brings spiritual consciousness into our lives. He encourages us to search for a larger meaning for our personal experiences and teaches us about faith as a way of deepening consciousness. Neptune is traditionally considered to be the higher octave of Venus, where her values and aesthetics are expressed at a more spiritual level through the imagination and psychic opening of Neptune.

Which brings us to dwarf planet **Pluto**, who is the gatekeeper of the outer transpersonal planets. Here we must accept the limitations of our ego consciousness, let go of compulsions and unconscious constructs, and accept that change is the only constant. Pluto dissolves our ego so that we can open to the new higher consciousness that is becoming available to us.

The discovery of Pluto enabled the psychological understanding of our lives. This produced the shadow paradigm, where the darkness in our souls is seen to be buried in our unconscious. The convenience of this is that we don't have to address it on a day-to-day basis. But we need to ditch Pluto's shadow paradigm to consciously enable him and these other new energies in our lives. As with all outer planets, Pluto manifests differently depending on our level of consciousness, so what we have been calling his shadow is simply how he manifests when we are at the personal planet level of consciousness.

As we get on the spiritual path, Pluto gives us the adaptability and resilience to mediate the transition occurring in our lives in each moment. And at the spiritually evolved level, we can transmute loneliness and separation into love and long-term relationships, effecting a regeneration in our lives.

Pluto now has two new brothers who share his orbit as well as his angle to the ecliptic. They also share his gravitational resonance with Neptune, as all three make two orbits of the Sun, to every three of Neptune's. Neptune is spiritual consciousness, so this orbital resonance tells us that the action of each of these planets is spiritual. Pluto's new brothers are, however, polar opposites.

The first is the seeker consciousness of **Ixion**, who enables us to develop our authenticity following Pluto's action to dissolve our ego center. We are one with the universe, but still exist as an individual, and that dichotomy is bridged by being authentically ourselves in our contact with the divine. Ixion encourages us to be a passionate, but lawless, follower of our heart, or loins, depending on our consciousness level.

Ixion is always encouraging us to ask the question, 'Are the rules we're playing by the right ones?' He urges us to push the boundaries and ask for forgiveness afterwards, rather than permission before. As we develop a spiritual approach, we enable our moral compass and learn to honor the 'bad' girl or 'bad' boy energy inside us and follow our heart. At this level, Ixion encourages us to be authentically ourselves, while being sensitive to the unspoken agreements in our relationships so we know how far we can go.

The second brother, **Orcus**, opens us to karmic consciousness. He teaches us to align with a spiritual creed and understand the karmic process of life. A creed expresses the shared beliefs of a religious community by summarising the core tenets. These tenants are simple and globally applicable, providing guide rails to help us navigate life. Orcus is Pluto's straight-talking brother. He is a master of integrity at the highest level, but at the personal planet level he can also encourage us to engage in double-talk and deception.

As we develop spiritually however, Orcus gives us a self-sufficiency that will nourish us through the long and difficult work that we sometimes find necessary for personal evolution. At this level, as we deal with the shadow side of our lives, we become accountable for our deeds and actions. And, at the highest level, we gain the shamanic ability to transmute shadow into light. Everything contains shadow and therefore presents us with an opportunity to transmute shadow, producing a new, more spiritual, whole.

Next, we develop higher-love consciousness and learn to evaluate our options with **Salacia**, who gives us the power to foresee opportunities and find the appropriate time to embrace them. She also gives us a self-protective quality that helps us weather both the real and the psychic storms in our lives. And she enables us to take a leap of faith, especially when we know we are going to be profoundly transformed by the experience.

At the personal planet level however, Salacia's liminal nature enables us to pick up on the sexual energy around us. We may have an erotic fascination or interest, and engage in socially unacceptable, even illicit, sexual activity. If this vital energy is blocked, we might feel out of control, or incapable of changing our situation. However, as we develop spiritually, she enables us to remove the barriers to happiness in our lives, and we learn to approach life with an easy sense of humour that helps us get through difficult times. And at the highest level, Salacia is about bringing true love into our lives and empowering us spiritually.

Then we embrace mastery consciousness with **Varuna**. We learn to devote ourselves to something so deeply, that over time we develop a sovereignty that is built on vast experience. We can look at Varuna as the higher octave of Saturn. Where Saturn rules by control and through laws and restriction, Varuna has a natural sovereignty, but we have to claim this through action. Sovereignty is a dance between our intention and the collective psyche. We have to claim it and at the same time others have to agree to give it to us. Over time, through this dance, we gain support and notability for our work.

Once we are on the spiritual path, Varuna teaches us to stand in the center of our lives and own the results of our dance with karma and dharma. And at the spiritually evolved level we can develop an inner conscious authority, as we learn to practice compassion-in-action. At this level, we are focused on the higher good and we likely have a mastery over the flow of consciousness in our lives. Indeed, we may experience on-going revelations and may become a sort of sage in some area.

Next, we connect to Source and embrace unity consciousness with **Haumea**, who works at a spiritual level to nourish and replenish our lives. She connects us to the psychic unity that exists across space and time, with the oneness of our existence. She does this in each moment by simply reigniting in us the magic of being alive. Haumea encourages us to live in the present and to savour every moment of life, allowing us to appreciate the beauty of the world around us, and within us.

Haumea is the higher octave of Neptune, turning his psychic opening into real psychic connection. At the personal planet level however, this can manifest as a lack of connection, a sort of spiritual alienation. However, as we develop spiritually, she gives us a direct link with the soul level and as we deepen our connection to Source, we learn to facilitate a constant renewal in our own lives and in the lives of others. At this level we understand that the bountiful universe manifests through us and we learn to enable this by leaving our ego at the door and trusting in the divine process.

Then we develop our spirit consciousness with **Quaoar**, who, in myth, sings and dances the world into existence.

Quaoar encourages us to find a practice to bring spirit into our physical lives. Song and dance are practices that call spirit into our lives, as are activities like meditation, yoga, bush walks, and even sport. Anything can be a practice to enrich our lives with spirit. Quaoar is also the song and dance we tell ourselves about our lives. Our unique song and dance is a spirit-story which underpins who we are.

As we develop spiritually, we learn to embrace a spirit of discovery, and to see life as a dynamic meditation where we can see opportunities in real time and act on them. At this level, Quaoar becomes the higher octave of Jupiter, lifting Jupiter's dumb luck into a smart luck through this meditation practice. At the spiritually evolved level, we see the song and dance of spirit in everything, and we understand that we are part of a rich chorus of spirit which underpins the physical world. This allows us to manifest spirit as required, to bring order out of chaos and create harmony in our lives.

Next, we develop systems consciousness and learn to innovate with **Makemake**, who drives spirit into our lives, opening us to the new richness of this sacred consciousness. He is a spiritual trickster, allowing us to play with the area of life signified by his position in our chart. He encourages us to see ourselves as an organic whole, as well as a member of a team. Through participation and understanding the teamwork process, we learn how to be sensitive enough to tune in to our fellow team members. This interaction gives us a worldview built from our experience, and a view of our place in that world.

As we develop spiritually, Makemake calls spiritual nourishment into our lives and gives us a devotional focus that borders on genius. We can look at him as the higher octave of Uranus, lifting Uranus' intuition into a rich understanding. At this level, we are able to alchemically break down existing ideas into their component parts and put them back together in new configurations. We understand the context behind the ideas, which enables us to be playful in this process. And at the spiritually evolved level, we can see the big picture and integrate it into our personal devotional focus at such a deep level that everything becomes a valuable, creative resource for our growth.

Then we learn empathic consciousness with **Gonggong**, who encourages us to participate in the marketplace of life. He enables us to feel inside other people and walk a mile in their shoes so we may see the world through their eyes. In order to empathize with others however we have to get out of our own emotions. So, at the personal planet level, he can encourage us to be emotionally self-indulgent and to lash out in an attempt to get our own way. At this level, we may feel overwhelmed by our emotions, and unable to see a clear path forward through the morass of our personal feelings.

As we develop a more spiritual approach, we begin to understand that we live in a symbiotic relationship with others, and that our divine work is to let go of the base emotions so we can be sensitive to the emotional community in which we are nestled and open to the empathic support of others. At this level we can pool our energy to achieve collective aims, as we learn to channel our emotions and mold our psychic space to improve our productivity. And at the spiritually evolved level, we can nurture the emotional and psychic bonds between us.

Next, we come to diversity consciousness with **Eris**, as we learn to value everything and everyone for who they are. Eris encourages us to simultaneously look at ourselves in an uncompromising way, and also be inclusive in our world view. We tend to fool ourselves and overlook our shortcomings just to get through each day, but Eris draws her strength from the unflinching nature of her understanding. It's all valuable to her and we'll only be complete and embrace our full power when we accept our multifaceted nature.

At the personal planet level, Eris encourages us to engage in discord and strife, so we learn to stop fooling ourselves, or stop being fooled. As we adopt a more spiritual approach, we understand that our strife can be dealt with simply by accepting opposing points of view. At this level she enables us to see clearly, without preconceptions, and helps us keep body and mind in harmony so that health and happiness prevails. At the highest level, she is a spirit-guide, transmuting life into love, and bringing sacred wisdom into our lives. Eris is the higher octave of Pluto, lifting his transformative energy into a fierce grace. This gives us a female power which is gentle, but which rises to meet the needs of any challenge.

Finally, we embrace the soul consciousness of **Sedna**, who is always trying to get us onto the spiritual path. She represents *Our Soul's Path of Destiny*. If we accept that our soul incarnates over a number of lifetimes and that it has a purpose to grow through these incarnations, then that soul purpose for this life is shown by the placement of Sedna. In that area of our lives, we transcended to a new holistic spiritual consciousness where we can allow love and harmony.

As we develop spiritually, Sedna teaches us to keep our heart open in what we are increasingly realizing is a sort of hell that we are currently living through. We are still very early in our consciousness development as a species, and we have to keep our heart open for our benefit and for everyone else's benefit in this difficult phase.

To enable this, Sedna encourages us to nurture our sense of humor. Humor is a wonderful tool on the spiritual path, because it allows us to release baggage and lighten our load on our soul's path of destiny. At this level, Sedna encourages us to beat our drum and sing our song to life. As we step up to do the soul-based work that we are here to do, we move through a fated transcendence to a more transpersonal consciousness.

At the spiritually evolved level, we can embrace our spiritual destiny and joyfully do what our soul wants to do. At this level she brings us transcendent peace, and the ability to nurture abundance. When we're in tune with our soul needs, our material needs manifest in our lives in each moment. It may not be what we want, but it is what we need. And, as we have the courage to embrace and nurture that, we open to the source of abundance in our lives.

Consciousness Workbook

Welcome to the adventure of embracing these new aspects of consciousness in your life! We see in our research at the Dwarf Planet University, how, by simply making these new planets conscious, students become empowered, and their lives are transformed. To do this we need to engage with these new consciousness energies, and by engaging, we take them out of the unconscious arena of action.

To enable this engagement, this book includes consciousness challenges for each planet. These are exercises to help us engage with these new aspects of consciousness, so we can on-board their energy in our lives. As we do, we will find ourselves becoming empowered and our lives will be transformed.

Several of these new energies, particularly Haumea and Makemake, remind us that divine matters are best approached in a playful way. Playfulness helps to remove the fear of failure in our consciousness adventure. There is no failure because all the data is valuable. It's only a failure when we don't integrate the experience, which means that the 'bad' outcome will happen again. However, when it does, it gives us yet another chance to get it right. So, I encourage you to be playful in your use of the exercises and ideas in this book.

Your birth chart is divided into twelve houses which represent different areas of your life, such as home, or relationships. The houses focus the ethereal outer planet energies so we can more clearly see them in our daily lives. So, for each planet you'll find house interpretations, showing how the planet's energy is likely to be expressed in each of these key areas.

You will get the most out of the exercises and the interpretations by knowing in which houses each of your dwarf planets are placed. In the appendix you will find directions for working this out in a simple way online. And, if you don't know what the houses are, you'll also find a guide to basic astrology in the appendix. While you will get more out of this resource if you put in the effort to learn your house placements, rest assured that you will still benefit from reading this book and doing the exercises even without knowing where these planets are in your birth chart.

Those with astrological experience might also appreciate reading the appendix on *Dwarf Planets as Higher Octaves* prior to embracing these new energies. A higher octave expresses an inner planet energy at a more spiritual level and this appendix provides a simple framework to understand these new planets as higher octaves of the planets we know and love.

Finally, bear in mind that these new consciousness energies manifest in our lives differently, depending on our current level of consciousness. You will find that each planet has been interpreted in each house, differently for those at the personal planet level of consciousness, which we'll call the unconscious level, or for those on the spiritual path, and also those at the spiritually evolved level. We're all working at all levels, and we are likely to see ourselves reflected in the interpretations at each level to varying degrees. The aim is to encounter the higher manifestations of each planet in our lives, which we do by developing our spiritual perspective.

And just a note that while we're working outwards in order as we encounter these new planets, and this suggests a sequential development in line with his cosmological order, our own personal development is generally a lot more of a multidimensional jigsaw, than it is a 10 step program.

Chapter One

Ixion opens us to seeker consciousness, allowing us to develop our authenticity and to follow our bliss. We are one with the universe, but still exist as an individual, and that dichotomy is bridged by being authentically ourselves in our contact with each moment and with the divine.

Ixion is the wild child in each of us that just wants to satisfy our personal passions and is constantly asking *'Are the rules we're playing by the right ones?'* He teaches us to foster an independence of spirit, which enables our seeker consciousness and allows us to pursue a personal spiritual mission.

He gives us the passion to be authentically ourselves and in doing so we will likely step outside the norm and push the social envelope. In bravely being ourselves, we may step on some toes and, to maintain our freedom of action, we need to practice asking for forgiveness afterwards, rather than permission before.

In myth Ixion has no sense of right or wrong and he lacks boundaries. What he does have is an inventiveness and a joy in life. So in our lives he gives us the strength to follow our bliss, even if it means taking the tiger by the tail to create change. We can do this secure in the knowledge that we have to break some eggs in order to make an omelette.

To enable this energy in our lives, we need to own the 'bad' girl or 'bad' boy inside us. Society and our upbringing have labelled certain things or actions bad, to guide us away from them, but they are likely just repressed energies that have been labelled bad. So the 'bad' boy or girl inside is like being ourselves without these inhibitions.

The secret to releasing these inhibitions is to become sensitive to the unspoken agreements in our relationships. Then we can sense how far we can go in each interaction. We have unspoken agreements with everyone, even strangers we pass on the sidewalk, we unconsciously agree not to touch them or look in their eyes. These agreements are different for everyone, and the grey area between our inhibitions and the unspoken agreements is Ixion's play-space.

At the personal planet level of consciousness Ixion compulsively urges us to disregard boundaries and take what we want when we want it, without any consideration for others. This is obviously going to lead us into trouble, which we overlook in the passion of the moment. As a result of this, we may not keep our promises, which can lead to retribution and eventually to an outcast, outlaw status.

Once outcast, we may receive a second chance and we have to embrace that opportunity and learn from our experience, so we don't repeat our mistakes. However at this level there is the danger that we will waste our second chance through the arousal of base passions. So, when we are unconscious of this energy, we may try and get what we want without regard for norms, and waste any second chances we may receive.

Once we're on the spiritual path, however, Ixion represents a passionate spiritual mission which may involve a violation of existing customs and a resulting catharsis, followed by opportunities for a second chance. At this level, we can embrace the freedom to be ourselves, to forgive our missteps and learn from our mistakes.

As we develop spiritually, our seeker consciousness is enabled and this gives us the strength to pursue our personal spiritual passion. This consciousness is what we need to pursue a personal spiritual path in this world, a path which will likely start by accepting our passionate nature. At this level, Ixion represents a passionate lawless energy with an ability to bend the rules to get things done and learn from experience.

As we reach the spiritually evolved level we define our own rules and live life on our own terms, while respecting the implicit agreements in our relationships and transmuting our base emotions. At this level, Ixion is passionate and spiritual, and able to maintain a personal spiritual path. The myth is all about a passionate personal mission and, with the orbital resonance with Neptune, at the more enlightened level this can become a spiritual mission, where personal passions can become spiritual paths.

Where Neptune's spirituality is nebulous, Ixion takes that energy and focusses it in a personal spiritual mission that is not afraid to experience both the dark and light sides and to go beyond the norms. We need a strong internal passion to guide us beyond the traditional ideas that are crumbling around us in the present era. Our world and our place in it are changing so fast that the old rules don't work effectively anymore, and we each need to develop our seeker consciousness to chart our own course into the future.

Owning our Bad Boy or Bad Girl

As with all the planetary energies, when we don't own the energy, we project it out into our lives and then we will call bad boys and bad girls to us. We need this energy of 'pushing the boundaries' in our lives so either we own it, or we attract it. And when we attract it we have no control over how it manifests. Generally it will manifest as undesirable people coming into our lives in the area associated with our Ixion house placement. For those experiencing this, see Exercise 3 below.

And a quick cautionary tale from the myth, for those who think that, because we need to let our bad person out, we can just do anything we want. Think again. In myth Ixion stepped over the line and was ostracised. Then he was given a second chance and he abused that as well. He was eventually bound to a burning wheel and sent spinning through all eternity.

So, if we want to avoid punishing consequences, we need to be sensitive about following our passion right up to the line, and if we cross it, learning from our mistake so it doesn't happen again. We need to be sensitive to both the spoken and unspoken agreements we have with others, so we know how authentic we can be in each situation.

Ixion Consciousness Challenges

We need to engage with these new consciousness energies to on-board them in our lives. So here are some exercises to help develop this seeker consciousness. They will be best focused in the area of life represented by your Ixion House position, as outlined in the following interpretations.

1. **Follow your bliss.** If you don't normally follow your heart, make an effort to *spontaneously* do something you really want to do, *when you want to do it*. The secret is to 'give yourself permission'. One way to do this is to declare a holiday and give yourself 'time off'.

2. **Have a 'bad' person day.** Set aside a day where you let yourself do the things you really want to do, but don't normally let yourself. If challenged, practice asking for forgiveness afterwards, rather than seeking permission before.

3. **Offing the others.** If Ixion is manifesting as disreputable others coming into your life, it means that you are not expressing your 'bad' girl or 'bad' boy energy. Try gradually letting yourself out to play by doing one of the things you secretly long to do. As you own this energy, you will find that there is no need for it to manifest as others pushing you to be authentic.

4. **Change the rules.** In the area of life represented by your Ixion house position, ask yourself, *"Are the rules I'm playing by, the right ones?"* And if they are not, *"Can any of them be changed?"* Take action to change any you can.

5. **Second time lucky.** The more we can learn from our experience, the better. Notice when you encounter a lesson a second time and immediately internalize that lesson, so you don't encounter it a third time. The third time could be the burning wheel.

6. **Pushing boundaries.** Pay attention to the unspoken agreements in each moment of your day. Each individual is different in their application of the general rules of behavior, and in their tolerance for flexibility. Then, when you feel it's okay, be proactive about pushing the boundaries where it is not going to be a problem.

7. **Normal / Abnormal question.** Here's an Ixionic street exercise to explore boundaries. Choose a busy pedestrian area and watch the people. They are all different. Many wear their boundaries on the outside and you can tell that they don't want interaction. After a while choose someone who looks approachable and ask them a normal question. *"Can you tell me the time?"* or *"Where is the supermarket?"*. If they tell you and move on, there is an unspoken boundary clicking in. But if they are hanging around and you feel they are open to more, follow that with an abnormal question. *"Do you like dancing?"* or *"What did you eat for breakfast?"*. For some the boundary clicks in then, and they will walk off at that point. While others will play along.

Ixion in the Houses

First House

At all levels, with Ixion in the 1st House we are likely to embody this independent energy in our essence. We feel that it is important to do what we want, when we want and to honor our own compass.

At the unconscious level, this can become problematic because Ixion was a loner in myth who was shunned by society for his lawless ways and so themes of breaking or bending the law, or of ostracization can manifest in our lives if we are not consciously working with the energy.

As we get onto the spiritual path however, this placement enables an independent spiritual investigation. Although many spiritual practices require submission and acceptance of a higher master, we must have the room to be ourselves and make the practice our own. At this level our seeker consciousness is able to catalyze social change.

Like Clara Barton, who was a trailblazing nurse who worked in hospitals during the American Civil War and later founded the American Red Cross. She wanted to create an organization dedicated to humanitarian aid in times of crisis, which revolutionized disaster relief efforts. At a time when women didn't even have the right to vote, her leadership challenged societal norms by promoting women's active engagement in philanthropy and social change, contributing to the advancement of gender equality.

At the spiritual level, this placement can give a unique sense of self, together with an awareness of the social norms within which that uniqueness is embedded. At this level we can lead the way by example and play a unique role in shaping the future.

Like German-born physicist, Albert Einstein, who is famous for his Theory of Relativity, which postulated that all observation is dependent on the observer. This is a very Ixion in the 1st House perspective. This theory revolutionized our understanding of space, time, and the fundamental laws of physics by introducing the concepts of curved spacetime and time dilation. It paved the way for advancements in technology, such as GPS, as well as furthering our understanding of the universe and the possibilities of time travel.

Second House

Ixion in the 2nd House gives an inner strength to pursue what may well be a rocky financial road. It encourages unconventional finances and many with this placement may end up working for themselves.

At the unconscious level we are likely to play fast and loose with the resources at our disposal, by not paying our bills, or cutting financial corners, getting involved in confidence schemes, or deceiving through nondisclosure, or through straight-out theft.

Like the former US President, Donald Trump, who inherited his money from his father, allegedly without paying the appropriate taxes. He is notorious for bankrupting businesses and walking away with large amounts of money and tax benefits, while not paying the bills or the contractors working for him.

Once we get on the spiritual path with this placement, we may be able to make a considerable amount of money, so long as that is the result of our individual spiritual passion. But we may also lose resources and maybe respect at some point. When we accept this and learn from it, we can make the most of our second chance.

Like former US Speaker of the House, Nancy Pelosi. Although she lost resources in some key legislative battles that did not go in her favour, her proven skills as a negotiator and political strategist, allowed her to maintain her leadership position and effectiveness in Congress.

At the spiritual level, Ixion in the 2nd House can bring an inspired understanding of how to work in the physical world to enable our personal freedoms and thereby effect change from within. At this level, we have a practical seeker consciousness and may set up social rules to assist this process or develop disruptive technology which encourages the independent process.

Third House

With Ixion in the 3rd House, we will be free thinkers. No-one is going to tell us what to think or believe and we will likely challenge established thought in some way. We may appear to know things in advance of others, and by the time everyone else catches up, we are on to something else, so we may be underestimated and overlooked.

At the unconscious level, this placement can bring undesirables into our lives as siblings or neighbors, who push us to develop our freethinking approach. It can also arouse some willful righteousness in our communications with others, which may alienate them and turn them into enemies. As we grow, owning the 'bad' boy or 'bad' girl inside of us will lessen the need for this energy to be projected to manifest as other people.

As we develop spiritually, our seeker consciousness is enabled, and we learn to follow our bliss in our research. At this level, we can use any second chance we get in our communications to deliver them more effectively, because we learn from our mistakes the first time round.

Like English naturalist, geologist, and biologist, Charles Darwin, whose Theory of Evolution through natural selection, changed our perspective on the world. He was raised in a freethinking family and studied medicine but gave it up to become a fanatical naturalist. Yet he struggled with the contradiction between the prevailing Christian religious beliefs and his scientific findings, only publishing his book *Origin of the Species* later in his life.

At the spiritually evolved level, this placement brings an evolutionary power to chart a new course for humanity with our ideas and through our communication. At this level, our seeker consciousness can catalyze the development of society through the pursuit of our independent ideas.

Like Polish astronomer and author, mathematician, and Catholic canon, Nicolaus Copernicus, who formulated a model of the universe that placed the Sun rather than Earth at its centre. In his 1543 model, the Earth rotates on its access each day and the planets revolve around the Sun. This is how we still look at it today, so he is considered the founder of modern astronomy.

Fourth House

With Ixion in the 4th House, our home will be a unique expression of who we are and hospitality, or the absence of it, will be central in both our birth home and in the home that we create as an adult.

At the unconscious level, this placement can bring undesirables into our home, and these people could be guests or other family members. We all start life unconscious, so childhood can be the time when these undesirable people and experiences come into our lives to push us to develop our independent streak. If we are still experiencing this as adults, it is important to remember that if we don't own the planetary energies ourselves in every moment, we experience them in projected form. So, owning the 'bad' boy or 'bad' girl inside of us will lessen the need for this energy to manifest as undesirable people and events in our lives.

As we develop spiritually, our ability to 'follow our bliss' through adversity in our personal lives becomes an inspirational public example that is likely to bring us the respect and support of society and keep us safe from any ongoing conflict or controversy.

We see this in Pakistani female education activist, Malala Yousafzai, who was shot by the Taliban on her way to school for bringing attention to the rights of women to education. Her family relocated to England to facilitate her recovery and protect her from further attack, and she has gone on to become a leading human rights campaigner.

At the spiritually evolved level with this placement, our home becomes our temple, and our personal story becomes archetypal. At this level, we can create an authentic sacred space where our karmic challenges empower our seeker consciousness and inspire others.

Like the Dalai Lama, who is the foremost spiritual leader of the Tibetan people. Born in a farming family in a small village, he was discovered at the age of 2 by the search team looking for the new incarnation of the Lama. However, he was held for ransom several times on his way to the capital. Then later, when China invaded Tibet, he was forced to flee to Nepal. Despite these difficulties, his followers are inspired by his resilience, forgiveness, and unwavering commitment to the principles of love and compassion. This message has resonated with people around the world, and he has become a revered world leader.

Fifth House

With Ixion in the 5th House, we will have a unique way of loving and we will likely have love affairs which fall outside the norm and allow us to explore ourselves. Or we could have children who play fast and loose with the rules and push us to develop a unique parenting approach. Or we could be creative in a willfully independent and avant-garde way.

At the unconscious level, if we are not embodying the 'bad' boy or 'bad' girl energy of the planet ourselves, we may experience love affairs with people who may turn out to be not what they originally seemed and, in the extreme, may even be sociopaths, or draw us into illegal situations.

As we develop spiritually however, we have both the creativity and the contemplative perspective required to learn from our experience. When we do this, we can make the most of any second chances we may receive, and our seeker consciousness is enabled.

Like American performance artist, musician and filmmaker, Laurie Anderson, who specializes in multimedia projects focusing on the use of language, technology, and visual imagery. She has consistently evolved by adapting her artistic practice throughout her career, demonstrating a willingness to learn and grow. She continues to challenge herself creatively and to receive critical acclaim for her innovative and thought-provoking performances.

At the spiritually evolved level our individual creative efforts can resonate so strongly with the collective consciousness that it leads to meaningful change. The rich story world that we create, or the unique real-world event or product we manifest, provides a frame or context for others to see and develop uniqueness in their own lives.

Like English mathematician, cryptologist and philosopher, Alan Turing, who posited that intelligence and consciousness are not exclusive to human minds and could potentially be replicated in machines. He is famous for what is now known as 'the Turing test' which evaluates a machine's ability to exhibit intelligent behaviour that is indistinguishable from that of a human. He is credited with formalizing the concepts of algorithm and computation with his Turing Machine which broke the German code during WW2, making him the father of computers and AI.

Sixth House

With Ixion in the 6th House, we are able to fill our days by following our passion in each moment and develop our own unique individual daily routine. This is the house of the services we provide and, as we develop, we will be able to provide a unique out-of-the-box service.

At the unconscious level we are likely to rebel against the pressure to conform in our routine or our job. At this level our attempts to develop an individual routine can be a reactive process of cutting corners and bending the rules where possible. If confronted and offered a second chance, it will likely be wasted, which can eventually lead to an outcast status. Again, we might project the energy, if we don't embody it ourselves, and then we are likely to find shady characters inhabiting our daily routine in some way.

When we're on the spiritual path we learn to turn our daily activities into spiritual rituals. At this level, we understand that every moment gives us a chance to be authentically ourselves, and when we act on this awareness we connect with the divine.

Like Indian spiritual leader, Bhuteshananda, the head of the Ramakrishna movement, who encourages devotees to integrate their daily activities, such as work and service, into their spiritual practice. He believes that by engaging in acts of service with a selfless and compassionate attitude, it not only benefits others but also helps us to purify our own heart and mind. He encourages his followers to see work as a spiritual duty, performed with dedication, sincerity, and ethical values.

And at the spiritually evolved level, this placement can give our seeker consciousness an individual service mission. We have an ability to see through the detail of each moment and connect with the big picture, creating a uniquely individual spiritual approach.

Like Swiss astrologer, Louise Huber, who, together with her husband, is known for her development of a unique psychological approach to astrology called the Huber Method. This approach views people as active participants in their own lives rather than solely influenced by celestial bodies. It sees astrology as a tool for self-awareness and personal development, which can uncover the deeper psychological motivations and patterns behind astrological configurations, and offers insights into personality traits, life purpose, and potential areas of growth.

Seventh House

With Ixion in the 7th House, we will have passionate one-to-one relationships that can run outside the bounds of social norms. With this placement we are able to see where we can bend the rules in our negotiations, and we can find the holes in our contracts.

At the unconscious level, however, we might feel more like a victim in this process, getting caught in the contract loopholes. Or we might be actively trying to exploit these holes. We could also feel like we have to take any steps necessary to maintain our relationships, even potentially illegal actions. Or we might experience this in projected form and find ourselves in relationships with shady characters. Either way, at this level, we may find that these relationships do not give us the freedom we need.

This is exemplified in the theories of American behavioral psychologist, B F Skinner, who considered free will to be an illusion. He saw behaviour as solely a result of reinforcement and conditioning, with no regard for internal mental processes, subjective experience, or individual agency. Because there is no room for free will or personal autonomy, his view is criticised as denying individuals the ability to make conscious choices and actively shape their own behaviour.

When we are on the spiritual path, we must live for something we feel passionate about even within the bounds of our relationships. This placement enables the development of our seeker consciousness through unique one-to-one relationships that assist us in following our bliss and allowing us to develop our spiritual practice independent of existing belief systems.

At the spiritually evolved level, Ixion in the 7th House understands the unspoken agreements in relationships that enable them to work. This placement blesses each of our relationships with a missionary like focus, together with a playful irreverence to the norms, which enables them to be the vehicle of our unique contribution. At this level, we will transmute our base emotions and may even forswear couple relationships because of a 'marriage to God'.

Like Florence Nightingale, who established the first secular nursing school in the world and is considered the founder of modern nursing. She perceived her calling to nursing as a divine mission, seeing it as a way to serve God and alleviate the suffering of others. She believed that her dedication to her work required her to forgo personal relationships and the pursuit of a conventional family life. She made a vow of chastity and saw this as a sacrifice she willingly made in service to her calling.

Eighth House

With Ixion in the 8th House of the occult and sensitivity to the spirit world, we will have a unique take on the deep mysteries of life. We can see beneath the relationship drama in our lives and understand how we can follow our bliss in those interactions. With this placement we will not be content living under someone else's thumb and will need to strike out for our independence sooner rather than later.

At the unconscious level however, we may cut corners and take advantage of the joint resources we hold with others. At this level we can have a passionate desire to fulfill our base emotional needs, with little regard for the effect this has on others or our relationships. Or we might experience this in projected form, where others use us for their pleasure.

This ability to play with the drama of our lives is exemplified in the work of Lucille Ball, one of the greatest female clowns in history. She became well known through her sitcom *I Love Lucy*, of which she was both the star and producer. Her mischievous and impulsive nature drove much of the comedy, and the show often highlighted the contrast between her aspirations and the realities of daily life.

As we develop spiritually, our seeker consciousness is strongly enabled by this placement and we will likely have a passionate interest in the spirit world, in the occult or in astrology. And within the astrological discipline, we will likely gravitate to the transpersonal planets and the new dwarf planets.

At the spiritually evolved level Ixion in the 8th House brings an ability to adopt a playful approach to weighty occult issues. At this level, we can enable a cross-fertilization of approaches into a new independent approach, so a new best practice emerges.

Like Dane Rudhyar, who was a French-born American astrologer. He was the founder of humanistic astrology, which brought together traditional astrology and Jungian psychology. This centered the interpretation in the growth of the person, rather than in the determinative effect of their life, which revolutionized modern astrology. He introduced and popularized many astrological concepts that were previously unfamiliar or less explored, and his willingness to challenge traditional astrological methods attracted people who were looking for new perspectives and approaches.

Ninth House

Ixion in the 9th House can bring a passionate personal exploration of a topic that is close to our heart. We know how to play by the rules, and we also know where they don't make sense and need to change. As we develop our personal passion, we may write, talk, teach, or lead others in a unique way.

At the unconscious level however, we may be more interested in bending the rules to our own advantage.

Or we could be too emotionally invested in our personal passion and, as a result, cut corners. We might proceed without authorization, or act illegally in some way, because we feel that 'the end justifies the means'. However, it doesn't in most instances, and so we may run into a confrontation with the authorities as a result. There is also a danger at this level that we may not learn from these experiences and may repeatedly cut corners, or get led astray by our base emotions, leading to stronger and stronger consequences.

As we develop spiritually, however, we can embark on a learning-based path where we learn from our mistakes. At this level our seeker consciousness develops by charting our own course through the traditional spiritual philosophies, taking on board what works for us from each discipline. As we do this for ourselves, our individual life mission may also inspire others.

Like Helen Keller, who became blind and deaf as a one-year-old. This gave her a truly unique mission to express herself, as she grew from a child who knew no words, could not hear others, and could not even see their lips moving, to someone who could write and even speak publicly. She was a linguist, motivational speaker and writer who authored 14 books and toured the world, giving talks which were an inspiration to many.

At the spiritually evolved level, this placement allows unique 'far out' thinking, coupled with an ability to communicate this unique perspective. Failures or setbacks are seen as learning experiences, so second chances are maximized and, through this process, we can become thought-leaders.

Like Mohandas Gandhi, who was an Indian lawyer who led a campaign of nonviolent resistance against British rule. He used fasting as a tool to mobilise people and pressure the British government. By subjecting himself to physical hardships, he showcased the contrast between the ideals of nonviolence and the repressive actions of the British government. His fasts were powerful forms of protest that aimed to draw attention to specific grievances or injustices, and his leadership and moral authority inspired people to join the movement.

Tenth House

With Ixion in the 10th House, we are likely to feel that we don't fit in the box being offered by society, and we need to learn to make our own way in the world. Over time, we will create a unique social position that allows us the freedom to be ourselves and acts as a catalyst for the development of new social norms.

At the unconscious level, however, this placement encourages us to get what we want in society without thought to the consequences. If we are in the thrall of our base emotions, this can lead us into some tricky, even illegal, situations. This is particularly true in our professional relationships where we may not respect the implicit agreements that underpin them and so act irreverently or try to take advantage in some way.

As we embark on the spiritual path and begin to transmute our base emotions, we learn that anything is possible, but not always right now. Our seeker consciousness develops through trial and error in our professional interactions, and we learn where the limits are in each situation so we can maximize these. And we also discover where we can break from tradition and foster our authenticity.

Like Prince Harry, the Duke of Sussex, who is a member of the British royal family. As a child he was referred to by his mother as 'the naughty one' of the family. In his teenage years, the press labeled him a 'wild child' when he was seen smoking cannabis, drinking underage and fighting with paparazzi outside nightclubs. More recently, he famously resigned from his royal duties to prioritize his wife and family.

At the spiritually evolved level with this placement, we can become leaders in our chosen field. We will likely approach our work with reverence, and there will be a corresponding reverence for it from the public. We may even become seminal influencers and inspire others to follow in our footsteps and chart their own course.

Like Gretta Thurnburg, the teenage Swedish climate-change activist. When she was 15, she decided not to attend school for two weeks until the Swedish general election in protest for action on climate change. Her youthfulness and determination caught the public imagination. She went on to deliver powerful speeches and engage in protest actions with unwavering conviction. Her authentic and unapologetic style resonated with people who felt frustrated with the lack of action on climate change from world leaders.

Eleventh House

With Ixion in the 11th House, we are consciously, or unconsciously, tuning into the human weather pattern around us and sensing what is allowable in this particular gathering of people. This is the house of collective consciousness and Ixion's placement here drives us to seek out groups where we play a unique role or have the space to be ourselves.

At the unconscious level however, we can play fast and loose with the people we know through our profession. At this level we are likely to believe that because we have got away with whatever shady activity that we have engaged in till now, we will always get away with it, so we learn nothing from experience.

Once we are on the spiritual path, however, this placement brings the same passion and willful independence to our exploration of consciousness, likely gaining both support and controversy from the community in the process. Here our seeker consciousness develops through experience, which may include periods of feeling like an outcast because of our independent approach.

Like Alexandria Ocasio-Cortez who is the Democratic Congresswoman for the Bronx and Queens areas of New York City. With Ixion in the 11th House, she has a lawless collective consciousness mission. Elected at age 29, she is the youngest woman ever to serve in the United States Congress. She is very progressive in her views and advocates for the Green New Deal, Medicare for All, a jobs guarantee, free public college and the abolition of U.S. Immigration and Customs Enforcement.

At the spiritually evolved level with this placement, we can make a unique and valuable contribution to the collective consciousness, challenging established norms and entrenched ideas and systems. At this level we are likely to be able to bring a bold new vision of who we are and what unites us, and so become leaders in consciousness.

Like American futurist, inventor, and author, Ray Kurzweil, well known for his ideas on artificial intelligence and transhumanism, which have inspired new ways of thinking about consciousness and our interconnectedness. He has presented a bold vision of the potential for human enhancement through technological advancements in biotechnology, artificial intelligence, genetic engineering, and nanotechnology. He believes that by integrating technology into our bodies and minds, humans can transcend their current limitations and evolve into a "posthuman" state.

Twelfth House

With Ixion in the 12th House, we will have a unique spiritual view and are likely to question the spiritual orthodoxy. With this placement our authenticity is our hidden talent, and the more we foster this, the more we can see through the fog of conformity that we find around us.

At the unconscious level, we might find we are living largely independent lives which are however alienated from a society which is omnipresent and seems to be always working against us. And we might set up this alienation by not respecting the implicit agreements in our relationships and by not learning from experience. Or we may be too passionately invested in our own point of view and too unconsciously blinkered to see what is really happening around us. This is the house of prisons and institutions, so there may be real world consequences for stepping over the line.

Like Australian hacker and activist, Julian Assange, who founded Wikileaks. He was accused by two women of rape. Then by the United States for conspiring to publish classified material on his website. He sought refuge in the Ecuadorian Embassy in London for 9 years and has subsequently been in prison for 4 years in the UK as he fights extradition.

Once we get on the spiritual path and start clearing our unconscious spiritual baggage, however, this placement gives us a rich field of activity for our spiritual growth. This allows our seeker consciousness to develop through a trial-and-error approach where failures are simply seen as learning experiences. At this level, our seeker consciousness is able to seed the zeitgeist and change the world.

Like Ada Lovelace, an English mathematician and writer who assisted in the design of the first mechanical general-purpose computer, the Analytical Engine, almost 200 years ago. She is considered to be the first computer programmer because she developed the first algorithms to explain how the machine would do its various calculations.

At the spiritually evolved level, this placement can bring an almost direct connection with the divine. We can become a channel, and the divine can manifest through our uniquely independent approach to the material world.

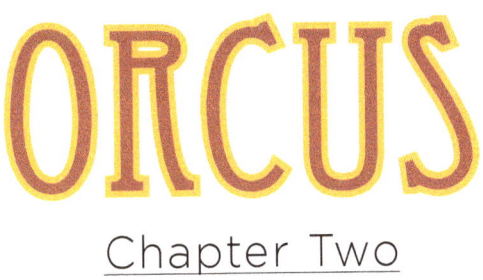

Chapter Two

Orcus opens us to karmic consciousness, the awareness that each of our actions has a consequence and he gives us the ability to see and deal with the consequences of our past actions. He teaches us to align with a spiritual creed and understand the karmic process of life. And at the highest level he gives us the ability to transmute shadow into light.

In myth Orcus dragged oath-breakers into the underworld. Oaths are contracts with the gods, and we call down a conditional curse on ourselves when we break them. So, Orcus is a straight talker, constantly delving beneath the surface to expose any corrupt dealing or two-faced activity that he discovers, holding us to account for our thoughts and actions.

We make oaths both to ourselves and to others. While the oaths we make to others are policed and have real world consequences, it is with the oaths we make to ourselves that we can easily fudge the line. New Year's resolutions are the social manifestation of these personal oaths, and we normally tell people our resolutions as a way of ensuring our own commitment.

When we are straight with ourselves, Orcus gives us a self-sufficiency that nourishes us through the long and difficult work that we sometimes find necessary for personal evolution. We are able to marshal the energy, reserves and resources to assist this process, we just have to identify and activate them.

He gives us a capacity to deal with the shadow side of our lives, which is all of our repressed tendencies that have been labeled as bad and stored out of sight. But they do us no good stored there, and in fact often undermine, or poison our best efforts. As we engage and work with this shadow, we can learn to transmute it into light.

The process of transmutation traditionally refers to the alchemical process of transforming base metals into gold and silver. So Orcus enables us to engage with the shadow through an alchemical process, where the constituent parts are transformed to produce a new whole. This is an active process with shadow as the raw material and light or energy as the result.

By encouraging us to undertake a deep investigation of this shadow side of life, to go beyond the normal limits and discover what is really there, we are also empowered to speak out and bring these truths to light. So, Orcus is the ultimate whistle-blower.

For those at the personal planet level, however, who are experiencing this energy unconsciously, there is a danger of falling victim to confidence schemes, or to corrupt dealing. These are two-faced activities, where 'what you see' is not 'what you get', and we could be playing either role in this deception, the one being deceived or the one doing the deceiving.

At this level we may be unable to keep our promises, and we may behave hypocritically, by saying one thing but then doing the opposite. And while, in the short term we might well get away with this, we inherently sense that in the long term we will always be held to account. We just choose to ignore that, telling ourselves the short-term gain is worth it.

As we develop spiritually, we become accountable for our deeds and actions, and we learn to align with some core tenets which provide us with guide rails to help us navigate our life. The development of this creed may come through aligning with the shared beliefs of a spiritual community, or we might develop our own.

At this level, we learn to understand the karmic process of life. We are born with certain givens, we have particular parents and live in a certain place, and these givens shape our lives. As we work with these givens, we find we are resolving some things and letting them go, and we are developing other things that are working for us. In this resolving and developing process, we create new karma for ourselves to deal with in the future. This is our dharma, the karma we are creating.

As we develop our awareness of this process, we increase our karmic consciousness and can assist and enjoy it. At this level, we learn to accept our shadow side as well as our public persona, welcoming the shadow encounters as important life lessons. We learn to upcycle these shadow areas. Upcycling is a process which takes something old and not working and lifts it into something new and useful.

At the spiritually evolved level, this becomes the shamanic

ability to transmute shadow into light. We learn to salvage the usable parts of the shadow and turn the rest into energy. There are shadow parts to everything, so everything presents the opportunity to transmute shadow and produce a new more spiritual light-filled whole.

Facing Our Fear

The biggest challenge with shadow work is facing our fear but, frequently when we do, we find that what we were afraid of was just an illusion. Our fear was literally just a shadow without substance, and facing it, or shining a light on it caused it to disappear.

Sometimes when we face our fear we find a real problem. This is where Orcus is really valuable because he gives us a persistence and an integrity, which isn't afraid to deal with the issue. When we embrace his energy we know that the pressure is best released, and that 'the problem' is actually a valuable resource for our growth.

This karmic consciousness gives us self-sufficiency in the face of our encounter with our own and others shadow sides. When we face our fear, we gain the confidence that we have the reserves to survive and the endurance to succeed.

Orcus Consciousness Challenges

Here are some consciousness exercises to help on-board this karmic consciousness into your life. These will be best focused in the area of your life represented by your Orcus House position.

1. **Learning from broken oaths.** Look at your last broken oath, to yourself or someone else, and ask: *"What shadow side of me got in the way of honouring my word?"* And when you find it, ask: *"How can I transmute this blockage into energy and light?"*

2. **Keeping resolutions.** If you keep your New Year's resolutions, you have an ability which doesn't have to be limited to New Year. Choose a simple attainable goal, and make a deal with yourself to make it happen.

3. **Marshalling resources.** Identify the area of your life which requires persistence and endurance and then see what reserves of energy or resources you can marshal to assist this process. Take it step by step, and trust that you have what it takes and that time is on your side.

4. **Finding a spiritual creed.** If you don't have a spiritual creed that guides your life and you want one, you need to find your spiritual community. The way to do this is to try some out - they are all open to new members - and see what suits you.

5. **Try an upcycle project.** Find an out-of-date and problematic thing in your life, perhaps in the area of life indicated by your Orcus house position, and find a way to turn it into something useful, to recycle it and lift the energy or add value in the process.

6. **Laugh at yourself.** If you have a long term shadow area which you have just accepted, you need to find a new way to look at this. One way we can do this is by laughing at ourselves, which is what we

do when we participate in any form of comedy. We think we're laughing at the comedian, but we are really laughing at ourselves. Laughter is a release of tension and when we laugh at ourselves we free ourselves from shadow.

Orcus in the Houses

First House

With Orcus in the 1st House of identity, we know in our heart that if we honour our word, even though the resulting journey might be long and arduous, we will have the reserves to survive and the endurance to succeed.

At the unconscious level, however, the ego-centred self-interest of this House might lead us to duck responsibility for our words and actions as we attempt to get away with what we can. And at this level we may be unable to keep our promises, behaving hypocritically, by saying one thing, and doing the opposite.

As we develop spiritually, however, Orcus's sense of exploration, coupled with the self-awareness of this house, teaches us to be accountable. We begin to understand the karmic process of life, and learn to accept our shadow side as well as our public persona. We might also align with a spiritual creed to help in this process.

Like British astrologer, Linda Goodman, who wrote the top-selling book, Sun Signs, which sold over five million copies, bringing astrology into the everyday market. She started a religion called Mannitou, which was an unusual blend of Franciscan and American Indian teachings.

At the spiritually evolved level, we are accountable for personal thought, word, and deed, and we can initiate the transmutation of shadow into light in our own life and in the lives of those around us. At this level, our karmic consciousness gives us humility in the face of our far-reaching spiritual work.

Like the U.S. Christian evangelist, Billy Graham, who preached to more people in live audiences than anyone else in history, reaching 210 million in more than 185 countries. Despite this iconic status, he was never ingratiating or pious, but rather earnest and quietly confident, always ministered from a personal level.

Second House

With Orcus in the 2nd House of self-esteem, we will have self-sufficiency in the face of the material challenges we face in our lives. This house asks us to be faithful to our values and Orcus asks us to be accountable. Following through on the deals we make will be the name of the game for our long-term success.

At the unconscious level, however, we might take advantage by not following through on our commitments when we see we can get away with it. We understand that the karma always builds if we do, but may still opt for short term gain, ignoring the long term pain. At this level, we could be blind to the consequences of our actions and there is a danger of falling victim to confidence schemes, either as the deceived party or as the one doing the deceiving.

Like German playwright and poet, Bertolt Brecht, whose operas and plays champion alienation. He was able to seduce everyone he met with his charisma, while unscrupulously cheating, using, and riding roughshod over everyone. He made a practice of publishing other's writing as his own, with some of his major works containing as little as ten percent of his actual writing.

When we are on the spiritual path, however, we can learn to see the resource challenges in our lives as tests of karma and with each new challenge we develop our resourcefulness. As we change our attitude towards possessions and value only what is spiritually useful, we will experience an increasing sense of self-worth.

At the spiritually evolved level, Orcus's deep-diving spirituality and everything out in the open attitude' combines with the generosity of this house to enable us to make a deep spiritual contribution. At this level our karmic consciousness fertilizes and nourishes the material world.

Like American author, wisdom teacher, healer, singer, and visionary, Brooke Medicine Eagle, who describes herself as an indigenous Earthkeeper and catalyst for wholeness. Her books include the Native American classic Buffalo Woman Comes Singing: The Spirit Song of a Rainbow Medicine Woman. Through 35 years of sharing her music recordings, teachings, writings, conference appearances, and wilderness spiritual retreats, she has touched the hearts and minds of people all over the world.

Third House

With Orcus in the 3rd House, we can delve below the constructs of mind that are based upon the convenience of our collective consensus to gain a deeper understanding of our world. We are able to bring this deeper understanding to light and so we may play a whistle-blower or a catalytic role.

Orcus demands intellectual independence and challenges established thought. And at the unconscious level there can be a resulting sense of intellectual persecution. At this level, we may have a closed mind, and not be willing to look at what's really happening, or at the inevitable consequences. We might also find ourselves getting lost in the detail and small bits of information, or assigning blame and finding fault in the ways of others.

Like American former CIA employee and whistle-blower, Edward Snowden, who disclosed details of a classified spy program to expose what he believed was excessive government surveillance of the American people. He was charged under the Espionage Act, and fled to Russia, where he was granted asylum and eventually citizenship, swearing an oath of allegiance. That same year, a court in the U.S. ruled that the mass surveillance program he exposed was illegal and was possibly also unconstitutional.

When we are on the spiritual path, however, we can develop the self-sufficiency and mental self-control to do our practice, day after day, no matter how arduous. We may also find support in aligning with a spiritual creed. At this level Orcus's sense of exploration can help us uncover a personal blueprint, or map that leads to a new and fuller understanding.

Like the former U.S. First Lady, Michelle Obama, who is a practising Christian. As first lady, she was a role model for women, advocating for poverty awareness, education, nutrition, physical activity, and healthy eating. In her book, *The Light We Carry: Overcoming in Uncertain Times*, she shares the *"contents of her 'personal toolbox' - the habits and practices, attitudes and beliefs, that she uses to overcome her feelings of fear, helplessness and self-doubt."*

Later, at the spiritually evolved level, we understand the power of words to shape our karma and our dharma. This karmic consciousness enables us to take old ideas and transmute them through our communication. At this level we may write and speak about this process and about the new understanding we have reached.

Like American psychologist and astrologer, Stephen Arroyo, who also uses Polarity Therapy and other methods of body and energy work. He is known for his ability to place the basic astrological principles in a current context in his talks, and for the ability to synthesise esotericism, natural science and psychology in his readings and sessions. He has a wealth of counselling experience and his books have been translated into around twenty languages.

Fourth House

With Orcus in the 4th House of inner emotional security, the more we explore our roots and heritage, the more confident we can be that we have the reserves to survive and the endurance to cope with anything, even in the most difficult circumstances.

At the unconscious level however the desire for comfort and security of this house, does not sit easily with the tests of karma from Orcus. As a result we might try and fake it when we can, by saying one thing and doing another. This is the house of upbringing and instinctive behaviour, so these will be crucial in determining whether we choose to fake it or to push ahead in difficult times.

When we are on the spiritual path, we begin to see the

karmic lesson in our heritage. And as we develop this karmic consciousness, we can start to work with the baggage we brought with us into this life. At this level we can accept our shadow side and transmute this into light and growth.

Like American actor, writer and playwright, Groucho Marx, considered a master of quick wit and one of America's greatest comedians. A recent biography insists his comedy *"is actually radical, nihilistic truth-telling that masks the great comedian's insecurity; its origins lie in his childhood, with his domineering mother and weak father, and his thwarted intellectual ambitions."*[1]

At the spiritually evolved level, we can consecrate our home as our sacred space and allow Orcus's revealing view of what we find there to move our soul. At this level we will be a master of integrity, challenging broken promises in our home and transmuting shadow into light.

Like American feminist pioneer and organizer, lecturer and writer, Betty Friedan, who wrote the best-selling book, *The Feminine Mystique*, which exposed the "desperate housewives" of 1950s America, women imprisoned in their homes with little to do. She came to believe that *"The only way for a woman, as for a man, to find herself, to know herself as a person, is by creative work of her own."* She helped to found the National Organization for Women, the largest and most effective group for women's rights, and served as its first president.

Fifth House

With Orcus in the 5th House of creative self-expression, children and love, we will be self-sufficient in these areas, and accountable for our creations. This is the house of risk-taking and Orcus's placement here fertilizes this process by revealing all our shadow material, which is what normally trips us up, enabling us to use this as a resource.

At the unconscious level however, with Orcus in the house of love affairs, gambling, and the pursuit of pleasure, we might duck responsibility in these areas or blame others for our own mistakes. At this level we may be unable to keep our promises to our children or lovers, acting hypocritically by saying one thing while doing another.

Like American author and talk show host, Rush Limbaugh, who used his status as an entertainer to avoid taking responsibility for the ridiculous and inaccurate things he said. He told his audience that he was always accurate and always right. Yet whenever he was shown to be wrong about something, he contended that he was an entertainer not a journalist and that, as such, what he said was never meant to be taken seriously.

When we are on the spiritual path however, Orcus gives us an understanding of the karmic process of life and we learn to be compassionately accountable. This is the house of teaching our passion and, at this level, sharing our discovery process could be part of our spiritual practice.

Like Scottish medium, Helen Duncan, who was arguably the greatest materialization medium of the 20th century.

Her séances were phenomenal to attend, she would fall into a deep trance and a white liquid, ectoplasm, would apparently come from her nose, spilling out onto the floor. From this, in about two minutes, a solid shape would appear of the deceased person, and this form, appearing quite tangible, would converse with their loved ones.

When we reach the spiritually evolved level, we develop the shamanic ability to transmute shadow into light through the unconditional love that is possible in this house.

Like human rights activist, Anglican bishop and theologian, Desmond Tutu, who rose to worldwide fame as an opponent of apartheid in South Africa. He popularised the term "Rainbow Nation" as a metaphor for the post-apartheid period, and since then has been active in the defence of human rights, using his credibility to campaign for the oppressed and to fight AIDS, tuberculosis, poverty, racism, sexism, homophobia and transphobia.

Sixth House

With Orcus in the 6th House of daily routine, which includes our job and our method of responding to everyday crises, each moment presents an opportunity for deep investigation. This is the house of vitality, health or physical sickness and Orcus's placement here gives the stamina and reserves to deal with any crisis.

At the unconscious level, however, we may try to cut corners in our work or daily chores, ducking responsibility and blaming others where possible, or just not preparing properly. There is also a danger of becoming involved in confidence schemes or fraudulent services.

When we are on the spiritual path, we find the courage in this house to understand the karmic process of life, accepting our shadow side as well as our public persona. At this level Orcus's spiritual nature and ability to deal with shadow gives us the strength to survive the tests of karma we experience.

Like the New Zealand entertainers, Jools and Linda Topp, known as the Topp Twins. The sisters are lesbian political activists, whose unique brand of entertainment has helped change New Zealand's social landscape. From their early work in the streets, they have grown their audience in a small conservative country to become well-loved cultural icons. Both recently received knighthoods for their services to entertainment. The producer of their documentary feature film, *Untouchable Girls,* said: *"One thing that stands out, is their generosity of spirit, always having time to meet their fans and give to many causes."*

At the spiritually evolved level, we are accountable for personal thought, word, and deed in each moment. This is the house of service performed for others, and at this level Orcus gives us the stamina and reserves to carry the load for others over long distances.

Like the American writer, Joseph Campbell, who was a leading authority and lecturer on mythology, the psyche and symbolism. His seminal book, *The Hero with a Thousand Faces,* reveals the journey of the archetypal hero shared by all world mythologies. He urged us to 'follow our bliss', saying: *"If you follow your bliss you put yourself on a kind of track that has been there all the while, waiting for you, and the life that you ought to be living is the one you are living."*[2]

Seventh House

With Orcus in the 7th House of one-to-one relationships, we will be accountable for our words and actions in these relationships, and challenge any broken promises from our partners. Seventh house relationships generally serve a functional purpose in society and involve some sort of contract. With this placement we understand this and can negotiate contracts that meet our needs and that don't involve hidden clauses.

At the unconscious level, however, we may see the holes in the contracts as opportunities, cutting corners and not fulfilling our end of the deal when we perceive this is possible. Yet this is likely to lead to quarrels, open enemies, and eventually to lawsuits: and if we do get involved in these confrontations, we will probably go to any lengths to win. Or we might not see all the ramifications of the deals we do, which can have the same effect.

Like an American actress, Grace Kelly, who became a big star early in her career because of her refinement, natural beauty and sexual charisma. She had many love affairs and the studio paid off journalists to keep her image pure. At the height of her career, Prince Rainier of Monaco proposed at the Cannes Film Festival, on the condition she stop acting, and that any children would belong to him should there be a divorce. She became the Princess of Monaco at 26, but the couple shared no interests, and the marriage was not happy. Frustrated, she moved to his apartment in Paris with her two unruly daughters and turned to alcohol.

When we are on the spiritual path, we can see the karmic consequences of our relationship interactions, and we learn to foster cooperative relationships. At this level we can accept both the public and the shadow side of our partner, supporting them and carrying the load for them over long distances if needed.

Like American politician and humanitarian, Jimmy Carter, who showed a deep commitment to evangelical Christianity from a young age. He became the 39th President of the United States, and afterwards established the Carter Centre to promote and expand human rights. His work earned him a Nobel Peace Prize: *"for his decades of untiring effort to find peaceful solutions to international conflicts, to advance democracy and human rights, and to promote economic and social development."*

At the spiritually evolved level, we can find a clarity and karmic integrity in our relationships, and we will likely have the shamanic ability to transmute shadow into light through each of our partnerships.

Eighth House

With Orcus in the 8th House of transformation and healing, we will be involved with a deep investigation of our collective energies and what lies behind them. This is the house of the occult and this placement encourages a deep exploration, and an ability to go beyond the limits to discover a blueprint, or map that leads to a new picture or understanding. This placement also encourages us to speak out and bring these truths to light.

At the unconscious level, we may have a sense of persecution for our ideas and revelations, or we may try to profit from our insights, or make money by not fulfilling deals and cutting corners where we perceive this is possible. But this is the house of karma so these efforts will come back to bite us, likely in the form of bankruptcy, losses and debt.

Like Argentine soccer champion, Diego Maradona, widely regarded as one of the greatest players of all time. His career began a slow decline when he failed a drug test, and he was suspended 3 years later when it happened again. He battled drug addiction in his post retirement years, then lost a lawsuit in an Italian court and was ordered to pay 30 million Euro in unpaid taxes to the Italian government.

When we are on the spiritual path, Orcus activates the occult ability of this house. At this level we have an implicit understanding of the cycle of death and rebirth, and are able to go beyond the limits of traditional belief or philosophy to challenge established thought.

Then, at the spiritually evolved level, we have such a highly developed karmic consciousness, that we gain a clairvoyant understanding of the karmic process of our life. This frees us from our karma and enables us to do the divine work we want to do.

Like American parapsychologist, spiritual teacher and author, Elizabeth Burrows, who was a well-known Christian mystic. In her early 40s, she said that she, *"entered into union with the creative intelligence of the universe, known as Cosmic Consciousness, or the Consciousness of God. And during the next few years she came to comprehend the total underlying principles of creation and evolution."* Shortly thereafter she renounced a personal life in order to assist in planetary evolution and peace. She appeared on hundreds of radio and television programs and is the author of several books including, Pathway of the Immortal.

Ninth House

With Orcus in the 9th House, where we search for the meaning of things, we will be engaged in a deep exploration that delves below the constructs of mind that are based on the convenience of our collective consensus, in an effort to gain a deeper understanding of life. This is the house of philosophy, of the higher mind, and with Orcus here we have the mental self-control and commitment necessary to get to the other side of any issue.

Yet, at the unconscious level, we are likely to seek the consensus view on these philosophical matters, aligning ourselves with established ideas. At this level, we may have a blind mind and try to duck responsibility for our word and actions, however, if we do, we will suffer the consequences of not honouring our commitments.

Like Australian politician, Pauline Hanson, who founded One Nation, a right-wing political party with a populist, conservative and anti-multiculturalism platform. In a lawsuit brought by a disgruntled former member, it was revealed that she fudged the numbers when she registered the party, and she was convicted of electoral fraud and sentenced to 3 years in prison. However, on appeal, the conviction was quashed, and she was released after 11 weeks.

This is the house of spiritual urges and of experience through exploration. With Orcus here we learn to be spiritually accountable, to understand the karmic process of life, and to accept our shadow side as well as our public persona.

When we reach the spiritually evolved level, the combination of Orcus's revelatory energy with the deep understanding and wisdom possible in this house, enables a deep spiritual self-sufficiency. At this level we may be able to provide visionary spiritual leadership which inspires and nourishes our followers.

Like Indian-American spiritual leader, Prem Rawat, the youngest son of an Indian guru who was founder of the Divine Light Movement. When his father died, his mother, elder brother and senior members of the movement discussed the succession. At the age of 8, he reminded them that their master was immortal and still amongst them. In response they accepted him as leader. At 13 he expanded the movement internationally and took up residence in the United States. Now in his 60s, he still tours and teaches constantly. He is a charismatic leader, who's major focus is on stillness, peace and contentment within the individual.

Tenth House

With Orcus in the 10th House of social responsibilities and professional career, we can push ahead in these areas through difficult times, going it alone if necessary and coping with even the most difficult of circumstances. This is the house of reputation and Orcus challenges established thought and practice, so we are likely to be known for this approach, and may take on a whistle-blower role.

At the unconscious level, there can be a resulting sense of intellectual persecution by the establishment for this role. At this level we are likely to find fault with others and assign blame as a way of dealing with authority or maintaining our social status.

Like American religious leader, Louis Farrakhan, who became National spokesman for the religious and political organization, Nation of Islam. A rampant racist and inflammatory speaker, he refers to Jews as bloodsuckers and rails against white supremacy with a uniform bigotry that includes Catholics, Gay people and Asians.

When we are on the spiritual path however, we can learn to be both responsible and self-sufficient, claiming our social authority and carrying our share of the collective burden for long distances when necessary. At this level, our sense of duty enables us to speak out on issues that are important to us.

And at the spiritually evolved level, we can transmute the shadow side of society into light, and may gain honour and social status for this work. At this level our karmic consciousness encompasses the community in which we work.

Like American actress, author, and humanitarian, Colleen Townsend, who was a noted member of The Church of Jesus Christ of Latter-Day Saints. Following early success in film, she dedicated herself to humanitarian work, specifically in relation to racial and religious discrimination, human rights, and in furthering the role of women in society. She partnered with her husband in ministry and served on the board of World Vision.

Eleventh House

With Orcus in the 11th House of collective consciousness, we are on a deep investigation involving our friends and acquaintances, the groups we belong to and our community, seeking out corrupt dealing, or any two-faced activity that we discover. This is the house of connectedness and networking and we have a need to belong to something bigger than ourselves, to a group with like-minded attitudes.

However, at the unconscious level, Orcus can give us a blind mind, so we may not choose the group very well, or we may get involved with groups that purport to be one thing and are in fact another.

When we are on the spiritual path, we learn to be accountable for our personal contribution to the collective consciousness, and call out broken promises from others.

This is the house of self-realization, and we might get involved with a group to help with this.

Like American spiritual leader and guru, Elizabeth Clare Prophet, who married a man who had founded a church based on Gnostic Christianity, Buddhism, New Age mysticism and Masonry. She had visions from her early youth and by the age of nine she had visited every church and synagogue in her hometown, seeking spiritual enlightenment. She realized she was intended to be a messenger while meditating with her future husband. Ten years later, when he died, she assumed leadership. By then the church had grown into a sprawling spiritual empire worth about $50 million, funded by the tithing of members. It continued to grow under her leadership until her death 36 years later.

And at the spiritually evolved level, we can develop self-sufficiency in the face of our long and sometimes exhausting adventure in the collective consciousness, knowing we have the reserves of love needed to survive and the endurance to succeed.

Like American astrologer and Sufi, Hank Friedman, who is considered one of San Francisco's foremost psychic therapists. He offers channeling sessions in which he contacts guides who he describes as gentle, loving, and profound. These sessions focus on present life issues and decisions, as well as past life themes, relationship questions, health concerns, and the spiritual path.

Twelfth House

With Orcus in the 12th House of collective unconscious and karmic debts, we have self-sufficiency in the face of the tests of karma, and we are accountable for our personal thought, word, and deed. With this placement we can delve below the constructs of mind that are merely based upon the convenience of our collective consensus to gain a deeper understanding of our own life and the lives of others.

However, at the unconscious level, we may duck this responsibility, blaming others for our own mistakes, or engaging in clandestine schemes, or in two faced activity, where what you see is not what you get. This is also the house of addictions, and we will need to be honest with ourselves about our personal issues to avoid these.

Like English novelist, poet, journalist, and translator, Mary Evans, who was one of the leading writers of the Victorian era. She wrote under the pen name George Elliot, because women writers were not given any credibility at that time. Her books include the classic *"Middlemarch"*, considered her masterpiece, in which she presents the stories of a number of inhabitants of a small English town amidst a political crisis. The novel is notable for its deep psychological insight and sophisticated character portraits.

When we are on the spiritual path, we begin to understand the karmic process of life. At this level the healing and forgiveness of this house enables us to accept our shadow side and to call out any corrupt dealing, or two-faced activity that we discover.

At the spiritually evolved level, we may have revelations, or align with a spiritual creed. At this level we make peace with our karma, and can gain the shamanic ability to transmute shadow into light, literally producing miracles.

Like Shivabalayogi, who attained self-realization through twelve years of meditation in a state of total thoughtlessness for an average of twenty hours a day. Emerging from this immersion and appearing before a crowd of tens of thousands, he emphasized the importance of proceeding directly to the supreme peace of self-realization, which he described as the goal of spirituality. He then travelled extensively in India and the West for almost 30 years, teaching meditation in silence through the power of his mere presence.

Chapter Three

The higher-love consciousness of Salacia gives us a deep sensitivity and a genuine love of life and humanity. This love enables us to weather both the material, as well as the psychic, storms in our lives, so she helps us handle deeply difficult and troubling matters more easily and gives us the capacity to bring something new into the world.

Salacia gives us the power to foresee opportunities, evaluate them, and find the appropriate time to embrace them: especially when the commitment feels risky and we know we are going to be profoundly transformed by the experience. She enables us to take the leap of faith required in this transformation, because we know in our heart it is right for us.

Everything is a process for Salacia. Processes are connected by the development that occurs along the way. Each part of the process prepares for the next part, so when we are in tune with where we are in our process, we know exactly what to do next.

In any process there are key moments where our interaction can materially affect the outcome. We know that if we make our move too early or too late it won't be as effective. Choosing the moment is more about allowing the flow of moments and seizing the opportunity when it arises. We have to be patient, yet ready to act. And we will know in our heart when it is the right time.

Salacia is all about intimate relationships and she can give us animal magnetism. At the highest level, this can bring true love into our lives. However, at the personal planet level this is more likely to be expressed through an erotic fascination or interest, or we could indulge in socially unacceptable, maybe even illicit, sexual activity.

At this level, we might feel that we are not in control or not able to change a situation. Or we might be so desensitised by the experiences in our lives, that we have an inability to feel pleasure. We could also be relationship-phobic, certain that we will be unable to find the right person and unwilling to make the compromises to make it work if we do. Or we might develop a practice of hiding, just at the right time, to avoid commitment or confrontation.

At this ego-centred level, we have a natural cunning which enables us to survive by being smart with our words. We might get involved in indiscreet talk and be unable to keep a secret. Or we could be prone to exaggeration, or the distortion of facts and visions, attempting to use them as a shield to keep us safe.

We could also project our issues unconsciously onto others, playing them out in the real world. Or we might find that others are projecting their issues onto us. As a result, we might feel attacked by our lives, and have to be careful of turning to alcohol to handle this overload because, if we do, we are likely to become dependent on it.

As we develop spiritually however, she makes us want to be better than we would otherwise be, and we may well experience a religious awakening. We could also be drawn to psychic phenomena such as hypnosis, telepathy, near-death experiences, synchronicity, or apparitional experiences.

At this level, we are able to remove the barriers to happiness in our lives, and we learn to approach life with an easy sense of humour and wit that helps us get through difficult times. Humour enables us to let go of shadow by being light-hearted. We learn not to take ourselves or others so seriously and this lightness enables a tension release which both protects us and assists our growth.

Timing is everything in comedy, but also in Salacia's approach to life. Timing for what? In the case of comedy, it is time for the audience to be ready for the next gag or line. But similarly in any other area, it is timing for the other people involved to be ready for the initiative we propose. At this spiritual level, we can sense the best time for each step of the process in which we are involved.

At the spiritually evolved level, our sensitivity can open us to psychic perceptions. At this level, we have the self-awareness to work with the unseen and take the leaps-of-faith required in our growth. Enthusiasm and emotional power are our hidden talents, and we may have a personal interface with the supernatural.

At this top level, Salacia is about bringing true love into our lives and empowering us spiritually. True love sustains us through its presence and constancy, giving us a tenacity and resourcefulness as we meet the challenges of each moment. At this level, she enables us to do work which will appeal to everyone and be popular even if it is confrontational.

Taking Our Leaps of Faith

Salacia brings us to those moments where we can see the change we are destined to be. And, if we have the faith in our heart that it is the right move, this gives us the courage to leap into each transformative commitment. We can do this because we know in our heart it is right for us and the outcome is what we want.

Salacia Consciousness Challenges

Here are some consciousness exercises and activities to help on-board this higher-love energy into your life. They will be best focused in the area of your life represented by your Salacia house position.

1. **Identify your choices.** Consider a process you are involved in as a whole. Then look at where you are in that process right now. Something is developing out of the work you are doing now. Identify the choices you have at this moment to advance the process. Play out each one in your mind's eye and choose the one that offers the most potential.

2. **Choosing the moment.** Patiently allow the flow of moments in your process. You know in your heart what you have to do, so you just have to seize the opportunity to do it when it arises. Cultivate an active patience.

3. **Develop your timing.** Salacia's ability with comedy and wit can be developed through games and training. Jump into any clown, comedy, or theatre improvisation class to develop your sense of timing.

4. **Study psychic phenomena.** Open yourself to the mysteries through working with hypnosis or telepathy. The world is infinitely more complex than we give it credit for and we can tune into that complexity in a myriad of different ways.

5. **Embrace higher-love.** To do this we need to lift ourselves out of the salacious side of our lives, out of love as a material experience, and embrace our psychic sensitivity and higher-love consciousness. Higher-love is not conditional or unconditional, it simply is and it embraces everyone and everything.

6. **Find true love.** This has to be the key exercise in this book and, spoiler alert, this is your life's mission so it can't be boiled down into an exercise. But we can say the Salacia way to do it is: Be open to the relationship opportunities while practicing higher-love, assess each of them realistically and take your time to make sure it is right for you. But when you are sure, take your leap of faith and enjoy the deeper meaning and support the commitment brings.

Salacia in the Houses

First House

With Salacia in the 1st House of self, we have an inherent sense of timing and a capacity to bring something new into the world. We have a strong drive to achieve our greatest potential and find true love, understanding that we will be profoundly transformed by this experience.

At the unconscious level, however, we may be too soft-hearted or mild-mannered to achieve this. Or we could be intimate with the wrong people, not understanding who our enemies are, or what their motivations are. At this level we could also be overly cautious of commitment and too hesitant in our interactions. Or we could be relationship phobic, avoiding commitment. Or we may have an extremely erotic fascination or interest, which works against the intimacy and love we desire. Our early conditioning may determine these tendencies.

As we get on the spiritual path, however, we can develop the sensitivity, appreciation, and gentleness to uncover our genuine love of life and humanity. At this level, we can handle deeply difficult and troubling matters more easily and we may experience a spiritual awakening.

Like British anthropologist and UN Messenger of Peace, Jane Goodall, who is best known for her 45-year study of social and family interactions of wild chimpanzees in Gombe Stream National Park, in Tanzania. She frequently speaks about her spiritual connection to nature and the interconnectedness of all living beings. She emphasizes the importance of respecting and conserving the natural world and the need for ethical treatment of animals.

At the spiritually evolved level, our sensitivity can open us to psychic perceptions, and also give us a self-protective quality that helps us weather the physical and psychic storms. At this level, we have the self-awareness to work with the unseen and take leaps-of-faith when required.

Like the American Christian mystic, Edgar Cayce, the father of modern holistic medicine, whose work grew by word-of-mouth. He gave over 30,000 psychic readings during his lifetime, giving accurate medical diagnoses and healing recommendations. He was known as 'the sleeping prophet' because he put himself into trance to receive these readings. Throughout his life, he did not capitalize financially or otherwise on his gifts. The readings never offered a set of beliefs or "religion" to be embraced, but instead focused on the idea that every person should test the principles presented in his or her own life.

Second House

With Salacia in the 2nd House we have the patience and the negotiating skills to find the perfect opportunity to achieve success. We have an easy sense of humour and wit that helps us get through difficult times, and may bring us true love.

At the unconscious level however, we might have a tendency to hide in order to avoid commitment or confrontation. Or we might have an inability to feel pleasure, and could be drawn to socially unacceptable, perhaps illicit, sexual activity to get our kicks. Feelings of not being valued might manifest as drinking issues or a need to address alcoholism.

When we are on the spiritual path however, Salacia's sensitivity can open us to psychic perceptions. At this level, we will have a talent for timing and can take the leaps of faith required for our material growth.

Like Canadian-born actor and stand-up comedian, Jim Carrey, who is an outspoken advocate of the "law of attraction". In an interview, he revealed that as a struggling actor he would use visualization techniques to get work. He also stated that he visualized a $10 million check given to him for "acting services rendered", placed the check in his pocket, and seven years later received a $10 million check for his role in *Dumb and Dumber*.

At the spiritually evolved level, we become determined and resourceful. At this level, enthusiasm and emotional power are our hidden talents, and we may be able to interface with the supernatural.

Like American theosophist, esoteric astrologer and author, Alice Bailey, who founded the Arcane School. She coined the term "New Age," so the start of her school in 1923 can be considered the birth of the New Age Movement. When she was 39 she met a spirit guide who identified himself as a Tibetan master called Djwhal Khul, and she wrote a series of "ageless wisdom books," which she described as his teachings. Her writing on esoteric astrology deals with the evolution of soul consciousness and the obstacles to that evolution.

Third House

With Salacia in the 3rd House, we will be gracious and sociable and have a genuine love of life and humanity.

With this placement we have a natural intelligence and mental subtlety, and are able to use cunning and adaptability to keep us safe. If we work creatively with communication, we may be stating truths in an inoffensive way using humour, or producing stream-of-consciousness, or emotionally charged, writing.

At the unconscious level, however, we may be prone to exaggeration, or distortion of facts and visions, rather than truths. We could also find ourselves caught in thinking patterns that cause us to project our fears onto others. And we have to be careful of turning to alcohol for support to handle the overload of life as it assaults us, because we are likely to become dependent and overindulge.

In the extreme, we see this in British musician and punk rocker, Sid Vicious, the bass guitarist with the Sex Pistols. He could not play bass at all, but sang and presented the desired image of angry angst. He and his girlfriend were heavily into drugs, and he stabbed her to death during one of their sessions. He was charged with her murder, but died of a heroin overdose before the case went to trial.

Yet when we are on the spiritual path, Salacia gives us a self-protective quality that helps us weather the physical and psychic storms we encounter. At this level, we are able to remove the barriers to happiness in our lives, and our ideas and communication may gain an almost universal appeal.

Like New Zealand singer Lorde, who is known for her unconventional musical styles and introspective songwriting. She self-released her first single, Royals, as a free download and it became an international chart topper. Her latest album Solar Power, features her in semi-nude album art. *"It is my butt kinda from below, and I'm in a bikini, so it's a little hardcore, but it was so joyful to me. It felt innocent and playful and a little bit feral and sexy."*[3]

At the spiritually evolved level, Salacia can give us the power to foresee opportunities, evaluate them, and find the appropriate time to embrace them. At this level, our work will be popular and appealing, and her sensitivity can open us to psychic perceptions and higher-love consciousness.

Like British psychic healer, Stephen Turoff, who offers psychic healing sessions to people seeking balance and well-being. He uses aura photography to capture their electromagnetic field, providing a visual representation of their energetic imbalances so he can provide appropriate healing. His approach involves channeling healing energies and directing them towards his clients to restore their physical, emotional, and spiritual health. Some clients claim to have experienced psychic perceptions or heightened states of consciousness during or after their sessions.

Fourth House

With Salacia in the 4th House, we likely have close family relationships and a graceful and optimistic attitude to life. With this placement we are able to handle deeply difficult and troubling personal matters and use these as transformative experiences.

At the unconscious level, however, we might feel that we are unable to change a situation in our home, or that something there is unsatisfactory. Or we could feel out of control in some way and so struggle to feel safe in our own home. And at this level, the privacy of our home may also increase the draw of socially unacceptable sexual activity.

As we develop a more spiritual approach, however, we embrace her urge to become better than we were before, and we make the sacred space to do this in our lives. At this level, we are able to clear the karmic baggage we brought with us, and work with the projections of others to mediate and facilitate our impact in society.

Like Scottish singer-songwriter, and political activist,, Annie Lennox, who achieved international success with the music duo The Eurythmics. Appearing in an early music video in a man's suit, she developed a powerful androgynous look and became a gay icon. In a later interview, she said: *"When you make a statement in your own way, people identify with certain things and they also project their own ideas onto you, and so I ended up with that sort of gender-bender label, which really wasn't what I was saying... (but) I had no objection to it. I thought it was kind of interesting that I was claimed by gay people as one of their own."*[4]

And, at the spiritually evolved level, we have a genuine love of life and humanity, born of an understanding of both our personal roots and our present needs and desires. At this level, we learn to ground divine wisdom through surrender to higher-love consciousness.

Like Dutch Indonesian spiritual leader, Pakh Subuh, who founded Subud, a form of Islamic mysticism in which the supplicant is initiated by means of a meditative communal submission to divine understanding. This can happen through silent meditation, through dancing and movement, through speaking in tongues, or whatever method of communion involving surrender to the divine that the applicant wishes to employ.

Fifth House

With Salacia in the 5th House, we are romantics at heart and we have an easy sense of humour that helps us get through difficult times. With this placement we value intimate relationships and we are able to bring true love into our lives, if we are rigorous with our relationship karma.

Yet, at the unconscious level we might be hesitant to take the risks involved in expanding our lives and, as a result, we might have a poor sense of timing, always a little late to the table. Or we could have the timing together, but undermine ourselves by drowning our sorrows in alcohol, or being lazy with our relationship karma, making true love elusive.

Like American professional golfer, Tiger Woods, who has a controversial private life. He is widely regarded as one of the greatest golfers of all time, however he crashed his car, amid reports of extra-marital affairs. Then he was arrested for driving under the influence of alcohol or drugs. He was found asleep in his car, which was stationary in a traffic lane with its engine running.

As we develop a more spiritual approach, we can embrace the playfulness and joy of this house to bring something new into the world. We learn to take the leaps of faith required in each moment to enable our creative evolution.

At the spiritually evolved level, we can base our evolution on higher-love. We have a genuine love of life and humanity, together with an idealism, which gives us popular appeal and the ability to playfully achieve our greatest potential.

Like American astrologer, mythologist, educator, and artist, Kelley Hunter, whose studies in depth psychology, cosmology, holistic healing, unified field physics, and spirituality have enriched her teaching and personal consultation work. She is a pioneer researcher into the meaning of our new dwarf planets. She also enjoys the creative process as dramatist, poet, and visual artist, and this led her to publish her *Planetary Gods and Goddesses Colouring Book*.

Sixth House

With Salacia in the 6th House, we have the power to foresee opportunities in our daily routine, evaluate them, and find the appropriate time to embrace them. With this placement we have a self-protective shield and can weather the physical and psychic storms in our lives.

However, at the unconscious level, we have to be careful of illnesses brought on by overload, or of turning to alcohol to handle any overload we feel. At this level, we might not take care of our daily hygiene needs, and this neglect could make us sick. Similarly we might not look after our intimate relationships and so reap the karmic results of that in our daily routine. Or we might find ourselves working with sex, or using it as a way to get through each day.

Like American exotic dancer, Candy Barr, who was sexually abused as a child by a neighbour and her babysitter. She ran away from home and became a prostitute in her early teens. Then she became one of the first pornographic superstars, starring in her first film, "Smart Aleck," at 16. She was also one of the most famous and highly paid strippers, as well as a playmate to gangster Mickey Cohan. She later emerged as a serious poet with her book, *"A Gentle Mind - Confused."*

As we develop a more spiritual approach, we can work through the projections that we feel from others and learn what is true for us. At this level, we can take the leaps of faith that enable us to provide a unique service to our community.

And at the spiritually evolved level, we will have a psychic sensitivity which opens us to higher-love consciousness. Our work is likely to be popular and appealing and we may have a personal interface with the supernatural.

Like Indian guru, Bhagwan Shree Rajneesh, known for the spiritual impact of his spell-binding lectures. Called the "sex-guru" because of his popular talks about tantric sex, his ashram became known for the open sexual relationships of his followers during celebrations. His commune in Oregon became a real-life soap opera of hedonism and murder plots, with reports that he advocated free love for himself and his disciples. Nevertheless his disciples loved his eclectic philosophy, much of which was similar to that of U.G. Krishnamurti.

Seventh House

With Salacia in the 7th House, intimate relationships are central to us and, at the highest level, we are able to bring true love into our lives. With this placement, we have an animal magnetism and are adept at sending sexual signals in our one-to-one relationships, but we may also chose to remain chaste.

At the unconscious level, however, we might be relationship-phobic, actively avoiding them or putting up false fronts to protect ourselves from them. Or we could be into socially unacceptable sexual activity, and use cunning and adaptability to shield ourselves from any consequences. At this level, we might also adopt a strategy of hiding to avoid commitment or confrontation.

As we develop a more spiritual approach, we can develop an easy sense of humour in our relationships that helps us get through the difficult times. At this level, we have a love of life and this enables us to remove the barriers to happiness in our relationships so we can all achieve our greatest potential.

Like American actor, drag queen, and television personality, RuPaul, who had an awkward youth, working as a go-go dancer and experimenting with drugs. He ended up homeless and broke. Then after a period of personal and spiritual overhaul, he emerged with a new sense of identity and comfortable with himself, saying: *"I'm black, I'm gay and I'm a man."* He went on to become the most commercially successful drag queen in the United States, receiving 12 Primetime Emmy Awards for his work on *RuPaul's Drag Race.*

When we reach the spiritually evolved level, we can bring true love into our lives and develop a psychic connection with all our one-to-one relationships, so that we understand them both in their depths, and in the play of each moment.

Like British astrologer and editor, Deborah Houlding, who is a consultant and writer, specializing in horary and traditional astrology. She gives psychic demonstrations, and has a background in mediumship, which involves co-operative communication with the spirit of one or more personalities in the spirit world.

Eighth House

With Salacia in the 8th House, we have the power to foresee opportunities, evaluate them, and find the appropriate time to embrace them. We are sexual beings and we understand the give and take of love that energises any relationship. With this placement, we could also be drawn to psychic phenomena such as hypnosis, telepathy, near-death experiences, synchronicity, or apparitional experiences.

At the unconscious level however, we may have a crudely-expressed sexual intent, and engage in socially unacceptable, perhaps even illicit, sexual activity. And, at this level, we may feel we have to sell out to get ahead, and we may be prepared to do anything to win the money or fame we desire.

Like U.S. actor and comedian Bill Cosby, who has the public appeal of this placement, but who used his wholesome public image to drug and rape young women who came to him for mentorship. He was eventually found guilty of three counts of aggravated indecent assault, sentenced to prison, and classified as a sexually violent predator.

As we develop a more spiritual approach, we can find a sensitivity which can open us to psychic perceptions. At this level, we learn to take the leaps of faith required for our soul to grow, trusting that everything unfolds perfectly for our growth.

Like Britan's Got Talent winner, Susan Boyle, who sprang to worldwide fame with her appearance on the show. She later said: *"I've a very close relationship with God, he's almost like a second father and I felt like he was guiding me at the time."*[5]

Then, at the spiritually evolved level, we can centre our relationships in true love, and find a divine contact that strengthens us and helps us achieve our greatest potential. At this level our psychic sensitivity opens us to phenomena such as telepathy. And we have a deep contact with the spirit world and with life after death.

Like Swiss psychiatrist and author, Elizabeth Kübler-Ross, who was an advocate for spiritual guides and the afterlife, and who also researched the phenomenon of near-death experience. She found that these experiences may encompass a detachment from the body, and feelings of levitation, total serenity, security, warmth, and joy. They may also include the experience of absolute dissolution, a review of major life events, the presence of a light, and seeing dead relatives. It is notable that these descriptions are similar to some transcendental and religious beliefs about an afterlife.

Ninth House

With Salacia in the 9th House, we have an easy sense of humour and wit that helps us get through difficult times. With this placement, we might use our intelligence and natural cunning to protect ourselves against storms and trials and we might create stream-of-consciousness or emotionally charged writing of some form.

At the unconscious level, however, we might be more concerned with outer expressions of our inner worth, rather than in nurturing that inner worth. And we could be into big dreams and have visions of being important, so we might have an overinflated view of our worth.

As we develop a more spiritual approach, everything we touch takes on a distinct spiritual sheen, and we may experience a spiritual awakening. At this level, like the fortune-tellers of old, Salacia gives us the power to foresee opportunities, evaluate them, and find the appropriate time to embrace them.

Like Stevie Nicks who, together with her partner and former high school classmate, transformed the struggling blues group, Fleetwood Mac, into one of the most successful bands in pop history. Three years after they joined the group, it was winner of the Billboard Group of the Year Award. Wearing chiffon and seven-inch heel platform boots, Stevie created her own gypsy-style look, swept the ratings, and made 50 million album sales.

And, at the spiritually evolved level, we can develop a genuine love of life and humanity. At this level, we can find a way for our ideas to appeal to everyone, and our work will be popular even when it is confrontational.

Like French American Astrologer, composer and musician, Dane Rudhyar, who incorporated Jungian psychology into traditional astrology to create Humanistic Astrology. His work addressed the broader human experience and sought to connect astrology with philosophical and metaphysical concepts. He also sought to bridge the gap between astrology and art, emphasizing symbolism and exploring the potential for astrology as a form of self-expression and spiritual growth. With an appreciation for beautiful intelligent women, he was married five times.

Tenth House

With Salacia in the 10th House, we are gracious and sociable, and we have the capacity to bring something new into the world. We have the power to foresee opportunities in our social interactions, to evaluate them, and find the appropriate time to embrace them.

At the unconscious level, we might be more concerned with outer expressions of worth and, as a result, be driven by these in our evaluation of our social and professional opportunities. And we could be prepared to do anything to win the social position we desire. At this level, our intimate relationships will be transactional, and we could be into socially unacceptable sexual activity.

Like American stand-up comedian, actor, and filmmaker, Chris Rock, who gained prominence with his edgy humour and quick wit, tackling subjects such as race relations, human sexuality through observational humour. He is frequently listed as one of the top five comedians. However, when he filed for divorce from his wife after 18 years of marriage, he admitted to infidelity, as well as struggling with a pornography addiction.

As we develop a more spiritual approach, we are able to take the leaps of faith required in our social role in the full knowledge that profound transformation is inevitable. At this level we are able to handle deeply difficult and troubling personal or social matters, and may experience a spiritual awakening.

Like American actress and singer-songwriter, Miley Cyrus who identifies as pansexual, and has dated men and women. Her chameleon like musical style is a wonderful example of Salacia. Her sexually explicit twerking at 20, on the MTV Video Music Awards, brought her 26 million YouTube views. She has said that the treatment of gay people in her church led her to a spiritual awakening.

At the spiritually evolved level, we can bring higher-love consciousness to all our professional relationships and our work will have a universal appeal. At this level we are able to achieve our greatest potential and assist others to do the same.

Like the Roman Catholic nun and winner of the Nobel Peace Prize, Mother Teresa, who devoted her life to the poor and sick through her service of universal love. She struggled with her religious beliefs, and towards the end she expressed grave doubts about God's existence. Yet, at the time of her death, the Missionaries of Charity that she founded had over 4,000 sisters operating 610 missions in 123 countries, including hospices, soup kitchens, orphanages, and schools.

Eleventh House

With Salacia in the 11th House, we will have many intimate friendships with people with whom we feel a like-minded kinship, and we are able to bring true love into our lives. With this placement we are idealistic and have a strong desire to achieve our greatest potential. And, if we are dedicated and sensitive to our process, we will likely have our wishes fulfilled.

At the unconscious level, however, we may have an extreme erotic fascination or interest, and engage in crudely expressed sexual activity which works against finding a true loving relationship. And we may not be in the right group, or have the right position in the group, to achieve our best, or to find that special person. Or we could use our position to take advantage of others.

Like former New York Governor, Andrew Cuomo, who resigned after the Attorney General found that he sexually harassed eleven women during his time in office, with behaviour including unwanted groping, kissing and sexual comments. One of the women wrote: *"I never thought the governor wanted to have sex with me. It wasn't about sex. It was about power. He wanted me to know that I was powerless"*[6]

As we develop a more spiritual approach, the hopefulness of this house and Salacia's love of life, combine to make us sensitive to the opportunities around us. At this level, we are able to remove the barriers to happiness in all areas of our lives, including our intimate relationships.

Like American comedian and talk show host Ellen DeGeneres, who has stated that she sees god everywhere. She starred in the hit TV sitcom, Ellen, in which she came out as a lesbian. The affection and openness of her impassioned love affair made her an inspiring ambassador for gay pride. She has won 30 Emmy Awards and 20 People's Choice Awards, more than any other person. She says: *"Heaven or hell is what you create right this minute where you are. You have a choice to live in joy or not."*

Finally, at the spiritually evolved level, we can centre in higher-love, and may develop a psychic connection to the collective consciousness and to the supernatural. At this level, our work will be popular even when it confronts the status quo, because people resonate with our commitment.

Twelfth House

With Salacia in the 12th House, we have a genuine love of life and humanity and an intuitive psychic connection in our intimate relationships. With this placement we can tune in to the zeitgeist, see the unfolding opportunities, and take the leaps of faith required to enable them.

At the unconscious level, however, we might not believe in ourselves, and might engage in superficial or secret relationships, or we may hide to avoid commitment or confrontation. Or we might not be in control in our relationships and might feel trapped. Or we could be into socially unacceptable, maybe even illicit, sexual activity, and this could lead us into a twilight world of crime. At this level, we may also have a tendency to project our issues onto others, or to fall victim to other's projections. And we need to be careful not to turn to alcohol to handle the overload we sometimes experience.

In the extreme, like American actress, Linda Lovelace, famous for the porno film *"Deep Throat"*. Her husband forced her at gun-point to act in the film. The movie earned $600 million, of which she received nothing. She was married to him for two years, during which time she was hypnotized, raped, sold, threatened, beaten and prostituted in a master/slave relationship. However, she went on to author two autobiographies, *"Ordeal"* and *"Out of Bondage."*

As we develop a more spiritual approach, we can work through our own and other's projections, and become our authentic selves. This authenticity enables loving relationships and helps us weather the physical and psychic storms in our lives. At this level, our work is likely to be popular and appealing.

Then, at the spiritually evolved level, we have a psychic connection to the collective unconscious, and are able to draw on both traditional wisdom and modern experience in our stimulation of the zeitgeist. At this level, we can foster the spiritual connections between people, and our work will likely have wide appeal.

Like American astrologer, Chris Brennan, whose study has focused on cross-cultural comparisons between the astrological traditions. He has a special interest in ancient astrology, specialising in the Greco-Roman tradition known as Hellenistic Astrology, but he also incorporates modern astrological elements, such as the outer planets. Since 2012 he has recorded a weekly podcast called *The Astrology Podcast*, which has become an industry mainstay.

Chapter Four

Next we embrace mastery consciousness with Varuna. We learn to devote ourselves to something so deeply that, over time, we develop a mastery that is built on vast experience. Varuna is probably the closest of the new consciousness energies to what we traditionally think of in the West as God, that all-knowing, all-powerful entity that exists silently behind everything.

In myth, Varuna is the god of the waters, which are our emotions, and he reminds us that they are deep and vast, and that we cannot change their nature. But he also encourages us that we have a soul of peace and love, and that wrath doesn't suit us. He is a king of gods, men and the universe, so he gives us supreme sovereignty. This sovereignty is power in its own right, without the need for control or support.

Sovereignty is a dance between our intention and the collective psyche. We have to claim it and, at the same time, others have to agree to give it to us. We start this process by stepping out in some way and saying, "I can do this" and then we have to do that thing and keep doing it over time, until we gain notability for it. Our persistence builds an audience for our work, drawing towards us the populace for our kingdom. The notability we achieve as we claim our sovereignty enables our deeds to live on in the collective consciousness, giving us a degree of immortality.

When we embrace our sovereignty, Varuna enables us to oversee the world and make impartial judgments. In myth he has a thousand eyes and he enables us to know what is true in any situation, and what is morally right. He gives us a desire for justice and the ability to understand the Divine Order. And, when we do the work required, we gain access to unlimited knowledge and become a sage in some area.

This unlimited knowledge can, however, blind us to the need to act in an immediate crisis because we understand that in the long-term, action is not in fact necessary. We know that the system will right itself. But this analysis doesn't factor in the pragmatic need to be seen to be in control. If we remain inactive in a crisis it can cause us to lose power or status. When that happens, others who do act will likely be given the power in our stead.

So Varuna teaches us to stay engaged when the body-politic requires it, or risk losing our hard-earned sovereignty. But he also brings the knowledge of when to 'let it be', when the other person has to do the work and there is no point in trying to do it for them. When people ask us to do work for them, sometimes this is part of our sovereign duty, and at other times we have to let them have their own learning experience. This pragmatic engagement between our duty and our divine understanding is at the heart of the dance of Varuna's sovereignty.

We can think of Varuna as the higher octave of Saturn. Both are supreme rulers, but where Saturn limits, controls, and structures, Varuna transmutes this energy into self-sufficient mastery. However, like Saturn, Varuna can place restrictions on us if we are not being true to ourselves or honest with others, but these dissipate when we forgive and align with Spirit.

If we are still at the personal planet level, however, he can give us an unfounded sense of entitlement which, when it inevitably doesn't work, shows us up as being incompetent and encourages us to blame others for our own shortcomings. At this level, we may be overlooked or demoted because of this incompetence, and we will likely lament our losses and hold resentment as a result.

Once we are on the spiritual path, however, Varuna teaches us to be sovereign. We learn to stand in the center of our lives and own the results of our dance of karma and dharma without needing outside support. As we develop this mastery consciousness, we gain support from our populace for the work we are doing.

At this level, we can develop our individual brilliance and talent through a deep devotion to our area of passion. We know that we are ultimately dependent on both our heart and the fire of our soul. We know the right behavior, so we are able to structure our lives, and be self-correcting in our endeavors.

Then, at the spiritually evolved level, we can develop an inner conscious authority and our work will inspire others. We know that we have a soul of peace and love, and we understand divine order, so we can relax into our sovereignty and practice compassion in action.

At this level, we are focused on the higher good and have likely mastered the flow of consciousness in our lives. We may experience visions and insights or have on-going revelations that inform our mastery. Over time we may become a sage in some area, someone venerated for possessing wisdom, judgment, and experience.

Laughter and Deconditioning

All of our experience has conditioned us to approach the world in a certain way, and much of that conditioning was out of our control and in the hands of parents, or teachers, or was just inherent in the society in which we were brought up. We carry this conditioning in our body as tension and in our psyche as fixed attitudes, both of which inform or control our every move.

Laughter enables the release of this conditioning. By laughing at our own petty habits and mannerisms, and at the existing social structures and roles, we enable a deconditioning process which frees us to claim our sovereignty. When we take ourselves lightly, we enable our mastery consciousness.

Varuna Consciousness Challenges

Here are some exercises to help engage with Varuna and on-board this sovereign energy into your life. They will be best focused in the area of your life represented by your Varuna House position.

1. **Claiming sovereignty in your personal life.**
   Identify something in your life which you would like more control over, and ask yourself, *"Who has*

control over this now?" Then ask, *"When did I agree to this deal?"* And finally, *"How can I change this deal to give me more control?"* Then start the renegotiation process suggested by your answers.

2. **Claiming sovereignty in the world.** Identify something you would like to do or offer, and ask yourself, *"What do I know well enough in this area to offer?"* And then, *"How can I start offering it?"* Choose your best answer, and do it! And be persistent about it, particularly through the early stages.

3. **Reverse engineer your notability.** We are all notable in some way within some community. Identify what it is that people look to you for, and reflect on how each person came to see you as notable in this way. Then cultivate that quality in order to increase it.

4. **Allowing sovereignty in others.** When people come to you for help, ask yourself, *"Is this my sovereign duty? Or is it best to let this person learn from their own experience?"* If it is our sovereign duty, we have to do it, but like the guru turning away the seeker because they are not yet ready to start the study, we also need to learn to say, *"I can't help with that, you'll need to do it yourself"*.

5. **Laugh at your own pomposity.** In a quiet space by yourself, deliver your favourite sales pitch, or a recent speech, or some wisdom you said to your friends, only do it in an exaggerated, larger-than-life way. If it doesn't inhibit you, you might want to record it on your phone and watch it afterwards, to assist the deconditioning process.

6. **Activate your thousand eyes.** We 'know' so much more than our mind will often acknowledge. When faced with a decision, open yourself to receive as much relevant data as possible from the world, and then trust your inner mastery to process it.

Varuna in the Houses

First House

With Varuna in the 1st House we can be the master of ourselves and, as we strengthen this sense of sovereignty in who we are, we can develop true individuality. With this placement we know that we are ultimately dependent on both the heart and the fire of soul, and by understanding ourselves and our relationship with the world, we can develop objectivity and independence of mind.

At the personal planet level of consciousness, however, we might overestimate our own brilliance and refuse to listen to feedback that contradicts our own vision of events. We might also blame others for our own shortcomings, becoming judgemental and moralizing to justify our actions. Or we might put others down as a defence mechanism.

Like British politician, Enoch Powel, who attracted widespread controversy for a "Rivers of Blood" speech, in which he criticised the rates of immigration in racist ways as he opposed anti-discrimination legislation. He was dismissed from the shadow cabinet as a result, but polls suggested that up to 82 per cent of the UK population agreed with him, and his views helped his party win the next election.

When we adopt a more spiritual approach, we can develop self-awareness, and the ability to laugh at our own habits and mannerisms. Laughter deconditions, freeing us from old baggage, and unlocking the visionary, insightful brilliance of this placement in the process.

Like American comedienne, Carol Burnet, who created the ground-breaking comedy-variety show, *The Carol Burnett Show,* which combined comedy sketches with song and dance. She created many memorable characters, each with their own unique personalities, mannerisms, and quirks. She was known for her physical comedy skills, including exaggerated gestures, comedic movements, and slapstick humour, which made her characters stand out.

At the spiritually evolved level, we can stand in the centre of our lives and own the results of our dance of karma and dharma, secure in the knowledge that we have a soul of peace and love. At this level, we have an inner conscious authority and can practice compassion in action.

Second House

With Varuna in the 2nd House we will have grand plans, insights and aspirations for our material needs, and over time we may develop a self-sufficient lifestyle. There could be a gain or loss of reputation in this process, which will either reaffirm, or throw into question, our sense of self-worth and basic values.

At the personal planet level of consciousness, we might lament any perceived losses, and hold resentment, relying on a mix of bombast, pompousness, and egotism to get us through. However, it is important with this placement that we honour our contracts to avoid what may otherwise be punishing consequences.

When we adopt a more spiritual approach, we can bring an inspirational vision to how we gain and spend our money, changing our attitude towards possessions.

Then we are likely to find that we have a talent for the cultivation of our income and resources, and the key to this will be our generosity. At this level, we can take a stand for what we believe in, and the sovereignty we achieve personally can change the world.

Like American civil-rights activist, Rosa Parks, known as "the mother of the civil rights movement" for her refusal to give up her seat for a white man in the black section of the bus. She said, *"I had been pushed as far as I could stand to be pushed. I had decided that I would have to know once and for all what rights I had as a human being and a citizen."*[7] Her arrest resulted in the Supreme Court outlawing discrimination on busses.

At the spiritually evolved level, we can learn to mediate between the cosmic order and the material order, regulating without force as required. The more we remain true to our values, the more material sovereignty we will gain.

Like noted German astrologer and reincarnation therapist, Baldur Ebertin, who received his doctorate in philosophy and psychology, with a thesis titled "Brain and Soul". His training in behavioural therapy, group psychotherapy and psychodrama, led him to become an esoteric alternative healer. His work helped people release past life trauma that was undermining their current lives. He believed that we have blockages, traumas, and avoidance attitudes from previous incarnations, including possibly hexes and curses, that we need to release.

Third House

With Varuna in the 3rd House we have a brilliance in our ideas, a talent for communication, and a strong need for intellectual freedom. We are likely also to have an ability to classify and examine information and a capacity to develop a comprehensive knowledge of the subjects we study.

At the personal planet level of consciousness, however, we might overestimate our own brilliance, and if the resulting incompetence is uncovered, we may try to blame others for our own shortcomings. Or we could get caught in thinking patterns, or lost in detail, and refuse to listen to advice that contradicts our own inspiration. Nevertheless, we likely have a doggedness about our dance of sovereignty which may well produce notable results.

Like American feminist pioneer and organizer, lecturer and writer, Betty Friedan, who started the contemporary feminist movement with her book, *The Feminine Mystique*. Her husband has been quoted as saying, *"She changed the course of history almost singlehandedly. It took a driven, super aggressive, egocentric, almost lunatic dynamo to rock the world the way she did. Unfortunately, she was that same person at home, where that kind of conduct doesn't work. She simply never understood this."*[8]

When we adopt a more spiritual approach, we develop the ability to laugh at our own habits and mannerisms, at our pomposity, thus freeing ourselves from unconscious conditioning. At this level we understand that our emotions are deep and vast, and that while we cannot change their nature, we have a soul of peace and love.

And as we deepen our spiritual sovereignty, this placement gives us a sort of sage energy. We know what is true in any situation, and what is morally right. At this level, we may develop a ministry and attract supporters through the reputation of our work.

Like Italian healer and Capuchin monk, Padre Pio, whose miracles numbered in the thousands. He developed bodily wounds in his hands, called stigmata, corresponding to the crucifixion wounds of Jesus Christ. Traditionally stigmatics have the grace of being able to be in two places at the same time. They also have distant vision, can read souls, and offer healing. The church restricted him to solo confinement, but people reported that he was seen hundreds of miles away, comforting and healing at different bedsides of the ill and stricken, at the same time that he was at prayers in the chapel.

Fourth House

With Varuna in the 4th House, our home is our castle and we will be the master of our domestic life, and secure in our inner emotional self. We are able to create a sacred space where we embrace our destiny with sufficient leadership that it impacts positively on others, bringing us to public attention.

However, at the personal planet level of consciousness, we could have an unfounded sense of entitlement, which, when it grates on other members of the household, encourages us to blame them for our own limitations. Or we could resort to being judgmental and moralizing to hide our incompetence in some area, and may suffer a loss of reputation as a result.

When we adopt a more spiritual approach, however, we begin to embrace the clues to this lifetime's karmic lessons that we find in our home. And we learn to stand in the centre of our lives and own the results of our dance of karma and dharma, regulating without force.

Like German politician and lawyer, Elisabeth Selbert. After women got the vote in Germany she wrote many articles and spoke at numerous events about women's duty to inform themselves about, and engage in, politics. She became a lawyer 5 days before the Nazis stopped women from applying. After the war she entered parliament and had a central role in ensuring that women's equality was included as a fundamental right in the German Basic Law.

When we reach the spiritually evolved level, we can create a sacred space where we can mediate between the two orders of reality, between the divine order and the order of society. At this level our sovereignty becomes archetypal and we lead by example.

Like the American author and Professor of Literature, Joseph Campbell, who was a leading authority and lecturer on mythology, the psyche and symbolism. His best-known book is *The Hero with a Thousand Faces,* in which he reveals the journey of the archetypal hero that is shared by all world mythologies. He believed that myths are deeply intertwined with our daily lives, providing a framework of understanding and a symbolic language through which we can make sense of our experiences, navigate life's challenges, and connect with the broader tapestry of human existence.

Fifth House

With Varuna in the 5th House we learn to master the process of 'being ourselves and enjoying it'. We may become notable for our creative self-expression, our affairs of the heart, or for our parenting skills.

At the unconscious level, however, we might bring a sense of entitlement to this process, and turn our lives into a drama by having affairs, or getting involved in questionable speculative ventures. And at this level, we might also struggle to collaborate and overestimate our own abilities, while putting others down and blaming them for our shortfalls.

When we adopt a more spiritual approach, we learn to stand in the centre of our lives and own the results of our dance of karma and dharma. At this level, we understand the deconditioning role of laughter, and we can adopt a more playful approach to the creative risk of each moment, claiming our sovereignty through successfully meeting each new creative demand.

Like American physician, clown, and social activist, Patch Adams, who founded the Gesundheit Institute in his home. Three physicians cared for twenty adults at a time at the institute, never charging money, and opening it to everyone. During the first twelve years, 15,000 people came through. For staff and patients, medicine was integrated with the performing arts, crafts, agriculture, nature, recreation, and social service.

At the spiritually evolved level, we can centre this sovereignty in love and joy, letting go of drama and allowing unconditional love as we embrace the spiritual joy of being ourselves. Through a devoted focus on something we are passionate about, we have likely developed a mastery in some area, which we might share with others through teaching.

Like Australian-English astrologer, Bernadette Brady, who worked initially as a consultant astrologer and more recently as an advisor, teacher and writer, winning awards for her "exceptional service to astrology". She is renowned for her innovative work to enlarge the astrological frame of reference. Rather than collapsing the planets onto the ecliptic in the way the chart does, she looks at their actual placements. She is also a strong advocate for the role of fixed stars in Western astrology.

Sixth House

With Varuna in the 6th House we are likely to seek comprehensive training and may build up extensive skills as a result. With this placement we have an individual brilliance or talent for the jobs we do and the services we provide, and, over time, we might prefer the sovereignty of working for ourselves. This is the house of wellness and healthcare, and Varuna is the patron deity of physicians, so we have access to a thousand remedies and the capacity for a comprehensive health understanding.

At the personal planet level of consciousness, however, our over-inflated sense of self might cause us to neglect everyday tasks like personal hygiene, undermining our health. Or it might cause us to bite off more than we can chew in our work, leading to a failure. As a result, we may be overlooked or demoted, causing us to lament our losses and hold resentment.

When we adopt a more spiritual approach, we can develop a mastery of all the tasks we accept and through the ongoing practice of them, provide a service which is valued and praised by others.

Like American novelist Danielle Steel, a prolific author, who often releases several books a year. Each book takes a couple of years to complete, so she has developed an ability to juggle up to five projects at once. Her books tend to involve characters in a crisis that threatens their relationship. All her novels have been bestsellers and they have been translated into 28 languages, with 22 adapted for television.

And at the spiritually evolved level, we understand that we are ultimately dependent on both our heart and the fire of our soul, and we are able to nurture both, likely gaining a notability for our work and the services we provide.

Like Polish psychic, telepath and stage hypnotist, Wolf Messing. He started performing as a psychic entertainer as a teenager, and became popular working in a circus in Berlin. His fame attracted many people who sought him out for his guidance. He explained that he wasn't reading minds, but rather reading the tension in the muscles, and listening to the breathing and the tone of voice.

Seventh House

With Varuna in the 7th House we have an emotional sovereignty in our one-to-one relationships. We know that we cannot change their nature, but that they are centered in the peace and love of our soul, which enables us to stand behind the agreements we make and master the tasks we accept in our partnerships.

At the personal planet level of consciousness, however, we might have an overinflated view of our own importance and put our partners down or struggle to collaborate as a result. At this level, we need to be careful not to judge or moralize in our relationships, because this will lead to quarrels, separation and lawsuits.

An extreme example is American criminal, Squeaky Fromme, who was a worshipful follower of cult leader and mass murderer, Charles Manson. To get what she saw as his 'message of enlightenment' on television, she attempted to assassinate President Gerald Ford. She failed in the attempt and was arrested, getting the publicity she wanted, but then spending the next 34 years in prison without getting Manson's message across.

When we adopt a more spiritual approach, we can laugh at the pompous habits and mannerisms that come up in our relationships, letting them go in the process. At this level, we can build cooperative partnerships and appreciate our partners as equals.

Like American actor, comedian, writer, and director, Tim Conway, who appeared in more than 100 television shows and films. He was admired for his ability to depart from scripts with humorous ad libs and gestures, which frequently caused others in the skit to break character while attempting to control their surprise and laughter.

At the spiritually evolved level, we will be sovereign and competent in all things official. At this level, we can develop true sovereignty within our relationships, drawing inspiration and support from our partners as well as being an inspirational support to them.

Eighth House

With Varuna in the 8th House, we understand that life is a growth process and we may have healing abilities, that enable us to find the appropriate remedy for any illness or situation. This is also the house of sensitivity to the

Spirit world that endows us with occult ability, and with this placement we learn to own the results of our dance of karma and dharma. We may become notable for this esoteric work and gain a form of immortality through fame.

At the personal planet level of consciousness, however, we might overestimate our own brilliance and mishandle joint resources, or wills and legacies, with punishing consequences. If we do, we might also blame others for our own shortcomings, lament our losses and hold resentment.

Like American attorney and then convicted felon, Michael Avenatti, best known for his legal representation of adult film actress, Stormy Daniels, in lawsuits against then U.S. President, Donald Trump. However he was indicted for tax evasion, fraud, and embezzlement, and was convicted of extorting Nike and stealing millions from his clients.

When we adopt a more spiritual approach, we understand the value of honouring our word and our contracts, and through this we learn to claim our sovereignty in these areas. At this level, we have a self-transformational force that we can invoke in our lives as we process our karma, and we can learn to master all the tasks we take on.

Like American politician, Elizabeth Warren, former professor of law at Harvard Law School. She supports worker representation on corporations' board of directors, breaking up monopolies, stiffening sentences for white-collar crime, a Medicare for All plan to provide health insurance for all Americans, and a higher minimum wage.

At the spiritually evolved level, we have the guardian of immortality in the house of the cycle of death and rebirth so we have an esoteric conscious authority. We know that we are ultimately dependent on both our heart and the fire of our soul, so we learn to practice compassion in action. At this level, we are focused on the higher good and we likely have a mastery of the flow of consciousness in our lives.

Ninth House

With Varuna in the 9th House we have a mental brilliance in our search for understanding and wisdom, and a capacity to develop comprehensive knowledge. With this placement we have talent, and a mastery of all tasks we accept, particularly in areas of culture, law, or higher education.

When we are unconscious of this energy, however we may overestimate our brilliance and refuse to listen to advice that contradicts our own inspiration. At this level we might get involved in issues of religion, ethics, morals, or law, and could find ourselves lamenting any losses and holding resentment.

Yet when we adopt a more spiritual approach, this placement is inspirational in a Neptune-like way, encouraging us to pursue philosophical interests, and explore belief systems, as we develop objectivity and independence of mind.

Like American poet, painter, essayist, author, and playwright, E E Cummings, who prayed for strength to be his essential self and to do something truly great. He was fiercely independent and eccentric, believing in love and spontaneity, which made him joyous and childlike. He wrote some 2,900 poems, two autobiographical novels, and four plays, and was widely regarded as one of the most important American poets of the 20th century.

And, at the spiritually evolved level, we can become a true visionary, sharing our insights through publishing or lectures, as we deepen our spiritual sovereignty. Justice, truth and moral law are important to us, and, at this level, we can develop a comprehensive knowledge in some area of life. We may even be venerated for our wisdom, judgment, and experience.

Like American professional astrologer, author, and lecturer, Demetra George, who draws upon her background in mythology and ancient languages to create a unique synthesis of archetypal astrology and ancient techniques. She is best known for her foundational book *Asteroid Goddesses,* promoting consideration of the role of asteroids in the interpretation of the horoscope, and for her integration of goddess mythology to illuminate the life of her clients.

Tenth House

With Varuna in the 10th House we have an individual brilliance or talent that will manifest in our professional career and the public areas of our lives. There may be both gains and losses of reputation through this process, but, over time, we can develop a position of sovereignty, likely embracing our destiny with sufficient leadership that it impacts positively on others and brings us notability and a form of immortality through fame.

At the personal planet level of consciousness, however, we might have inflated ideas about our brilliance, and so put others down and refuse to listen to advice. If we can't live up to our inflated ideas, we may be overlooked or demoted, and we will likely lament our losses and hold resentment as a result. However, if our inflated ideas are successful, we will be able to achieve great things.

Like Canadian-American businesswoman, Elizabeth Arden, who started with $6,000 in borrowed money and from that modest beginning built a cosmetics empire, with 150 salons in Europe and the United States. She was the sole owner, and at the peak of her career, she was one of the wealthiest women in the world. While before makeup had often been associated with lower classes and prostitutes, she was largely responsible for establishing it as proper and appropriate, even necessary, for a ladylike image.

When we adopt a more spiritual approach, we understand the deconditioning value of humour in freeing us both from tradition and from our personal habits. Through this we can develop objectivity and independence of mind. At this level, we learn to stand in the centre of our lives and own the results of our dance of karma and dharma without needing outside support.

At the spiritually evolved level, we can deepen this sovereignty and become a true leader, learning to mediate between the cosmic order and the social order. At this level, we will likely feel a calling to a higher purpose, believing that life should be useful and good.

Like the Tibetan supreme spiritual ruler, the Dalai Lama, who was discovered as a two year old and proclaimed to be the reborn soul of the Buddha of Compassion. He was given political and religious authority at the age of 15, when he fled from his native Tibet as it was invaded by Chinese communists. He now travels worldwide teaching Buddhism and meeting with world leaders, religious leaders, philosophers, and scientists. Since he won the Nobel Peace Prize for his work, his Kalachakra teachings and initiations have become international events.

Eleventh House

With Varuna in the 11th House we can live out our aspirations, and the transformational work that we do in the collective consciousness will bring us increasing benefits and wealth. The more we embrace our destiny, the more it will impact on others and bring us to public attention, and we may gain a form of immortality through fame in this process.

At the personal planet level of consciousness, however, we have to be careful not to come from a place of bombast, pompousness, or egotism, because then we will be poor at the collaboration required for our work to be effective. At this level, it is all about the gain and loss of reputation, and we need to be able to stand behind our actions to benefit over time.

When we adopt a more spiritual approach, this placement provides a powerful tool to assess our socio-cultural reality from a more independent perspective and free ourselves from prejudice and conditioning. We are able to play with the conditioning which our tradition has more or less forced upon our consciousness and see what really works.

Like American radio and television personality, Rachel Maddow, who was the first openly lesbian anchor to host a major prime-time news program in the United States. She has said that her show's mission is to *"increase the amount of useful information in the world"*. She received the Interfaith Alliance's Faith and Freedom Award in 2010, for her *"passionate coverage of the intersection of religion and politics"*.

As we deepen our spiritual sovereignty and centre in love, this placement brings insights and visions drawn from our interconnectedness, along with an ability to regulate and communicate these connections. At this level, the value of our consciousness work will bring us notability and a degree of immortality.

Like seventeenth century English astrologer William Lilly, whose book, Christian Astrology, is one of the classic texts for the study of traditional astrology. It remains popular today and has never gone out-of-print. A republication in 1985 brought about a renaissance in astrological scholarship in North America and Europe, and also a transformation of the techniques of modern astrology.

Twelfth House

With Varuna in the 12th House we are able to mediate between the zeitgeist, the collective unconscious, and our personal everyday world. We have a force we can invoke to help us release unconscious baggage and find sovereignty in the present moment, and we might have a hidden mastery.

At the personal planet level of consciousness, however, we might have a rich private world, but have difficulty mediating that with the collective. An inflated self-image, or a sense of entitlement, will complicate the process. We need to be careful not to hold onto resentment, or lament our losses and blame others for our own shortcomings.

When we adopt a more spiritual approach, we can laugh at both our socio-cultural reality and at our own pompousness, thus freeing ourselves from prejudice and social conditioning. At this level, we learn to take a more eternal view, and to value our karmic debts as spiritual lessons.

Like American artist, Jeff Koons, recognized for his pop culture work. He is famous for his sculptures depicting everyday objects, such as balloon animals produced in stainless steel with mirror-finish surfaces. His works have sold at auction at record auction prices for a living artist. While some dismiss it as kitsch, crass, and based on cynical self-merchandising, he has said, *"What I hope to accomplish with my work is to have a dialogue about eternal life and the external world"*.[9]

At the spiritually evolved level, we understand that consciousness is deep and vast, and that we have a soul of peace and love. At this level, we are able to inspire this spiritual realisation in others and we may experience visions or revelations, and have a talent for healing.

Like the Catholic saint, Maria Quattrocchi, who was beatified, along with her husband, for their devout life and for opening their home to refugees during World War Two. It was the first time in church history that a woman and her husband were given that honour together, as exemplars of Christian life.

Chapter Five

Haumea is the planet of rebirth who works at a spiritual level to nourish and replenish our lives. She connects us to the psychic unity that exists across space and time, with the oneness of our existence, and she does this in each moment simply through the magic of being alive. She encourages us to live in the present and to savour every moment of life, allowing us to appreciate the beauty of the world around us, and within us.

Representing a psychic shift from the world view that separates us from Nature, to the embodied recognition and power of being one with Nature, Haumea gives us the power to create and regenerate our lives when we align with the natural world and its rhythms. When we connect with our psychic centre, we are able to protect those we love, and we can embody the divinity in each moment. Her love is all-encompassing and unconditional, but to enable this we have to leave our ego at the door.

We can think of her as the higher octave of Neptune, where Neptune's psychic opening has the potential to blossom into a real psychic connection with Haumea, a connection to the soul level. We often understand soul on the individual level, yet when we have evolved and embraced Haumea in our lives, the soul level includes not only all of humanity but all beings. We are all one.

Life is a process for Haumea, a process of rejuvenation. She is always catalyzing rebirth in our lives. She does this by encouraging a spirit of play within the sacred work we are doing. Play requires trust in the bigger picture. We need to allow ourselves to let go and explore the myriad of creative possibilities without judgment, and that way we deepen the sacred. So her energy is playful and creative, symbolizing a constant renewal and a joy in life.

When we experience Haumea's psychic connection unconsciously, however, it can come with a similar righteousness to Neptune, but with much more psychic force behind it. As a result, we may ride roughshod over everyone, or stick our neck out about something and so get ourselves into trouble. So, she also talks of the day-to-day pressures we experience that might reshape us, and of the danger that it might all spin out of control.

Or, even more likely, we find no connection to the psychic source, so our life shrivels up and we live in a sort of spiritual starvation, a starvation of life energy. At the unconscious level, we are likely to try to fill this lack of meaningful connection by indulging in the hollow pleasures of consumer society. But no amount of money can buy the connection we seek, so this just leaves us feeling even more alienated.

At this level, we may respond by being overly dramatic and attention-seeking, or by making claims of martyrdom. We become so desperate for meaningful connection that we will go to any lengths to achieve it. And there is always a danger our drama could spin out of control and bring everything in our lives crashing down.

As we develop a more spiritual approach, we learn to trust in the life process and deepen our connection to the psyche through allowing the magic-of-being in each moment. We all know those special moments when we are out in nature, or in the arms of our love, or deep in meditation, where we feel the lifeforce chorusing through us. This psychic connection to the oneness-of-life is the magic that Haumea opens us to in each moment.

With Haumea there are times that we might pick up too much psychic energy and need to withdraw, absorb, and refresh through rest, meditation, or sleep. With awareness and application, we can learn to offload the non-nutritive more readily and connect with a never-failing source of psychic sustenance.

Haumea talks about being part of a family born of a collision with reality, and she teaches us the value of nurturing the disparate aspects of our psychic identity. She throws us into experiences where we collide with consensus reality, but in that collision, we find a like-hearted community. In these situations, we experience our shared interests, which creates a sense of family that transcends biology.

Thus, at the spiritual level, she encourages us to find our community, to connect with a family of souls who can play important roles in our lives, and to find a new way of living together with them. These people may be spread across the planet and may not be the obvious choice, but our connection with them will psychically nourish us and them.

In today's world where many of us are seeking a sense of belonging, of connection to land or place, Haumea also talks about migration to a new home. We have increased levels of migration from political persecution and accelerating global climate change, and Haumea is here to remind us of what joins us together. Her spirituality is inherent in the embodied experience. It transcends the dualistic mind of black or white, right or wrong, belief or non-belief. We simply know in our bones that we are interconnected.

And, as we deepen this contact with Source, we learn to facilitate a constant renewal in our own lives and in other's lives through this connection. We learn to ride the psychic waves and the lava flows that arise in each moment, and to be accepting and creative with those opportunities. At this level, we understand that the bountiful universe manifests through us when we are open to it. And, to enable this, we know that we have to leave our ego behind and trust in the divine process.

Letting Go of the Old

Haumea is always bringing renewal into our lives, but we have to welcome this and gracefully surrender the old, so there is space for the new to grow. However, our sense of security often derives from the possessions and routines that we have built up over many years and, as a result we can become very attached to the old.

When we are rooted in the past for our security, we protect ourselves from any regeneration because we fear it will challenge the foundations of our world. But regeneration is essential for a healthy life, as no living thing can maintain a stasis without growth. So, we have to be open to the growth, welcome it, and nurture it.

When we hang on blindly to the old, the only way the new can be birthed is through crisis and disaster.
By desperately hanging onto the past, we are actually calling crisis and disaster into our lives to help us let go and allow the necessary rebirth. When we cling, we are choosing to ignore the signals that change is required.

At any time, some part of our reality is obsolete, or creaking in some way, and new psychic opportunities are germinating. The challenge is to open ourselves to this germination and deal with the creaking piece of reality at the same time. If we trust that this is a natural growth process, we can gracefully surrender the old and simultaneously embrace the new.

Haumea Consciousness Challenges

Here are some consciousness exercises to help on-board this connection to Source into your life. They will be best focused in the area of your life represented by your Haumea House position.

1. **Take time-out to refresh.** Spend a day in your favorite nature haunt or, if you don't have one, plan an outing where you can immerse yourself in nature, and just relax into oneness with the energy of life.

2. **Find spiritual meaning.** If you feel spiritually alienated, give yourself permission to do something meaningful for you, no matter how weird or unproductive that may be in your normal terms.

Follow your heart into a psychic connection and enjoy the rejuvenation that comes from that.

3. **Find meaning through creativity.** Another way to find spiritual meaning is to make a piece of art or start a creative project. The playful nature of creative work helps us access the divine in each moment. Neither the product, nor our skill level is important, because we connect with our psychic center in the act of creation.

4. **Identify your collision family.** We all have a family of souls who play important roles in our lives and whose interconnection psychically nourishes us and them. Identify who these people are and nurture those connections. If you find you don't have any, seek out a collision with a like-hearted community.

5. **Learn not to call crisis into your life.** If you find you are hanging onto the old and therefore calling crisis into your life to enable change, something in your reality will be creaking in some way. Identify that. Then find something that is germinating at the same time. Nurture the germination and find a way to make the space for it, releasing the creaking part, or letting it decompose into nourishment for the germination.

6. **Honor your psychic connection.** If you feel a psychic connection, or it feels like you are receiving psychic messages, honor that connection to Source by acting on the messages, just as we do with intuitions. If they are not clear, write them down as a way of clarifying them. It is your interpretation which is crucial however, and it's you who has the connection, so ask: *"What does it mean to me?"*

Haumea in the Houses

First House

Haumea's psychic connection in the 1st House is to the center of ourselves. Planets in this house influence our personality and with Haumea here the 'magic of being' infuses our body and our views on life with a rich creative energy.

At the personal planet level of consciousness, however, this can manifest as an extremely egocentric approach. And because this house is about how others perceive us, we may come across as being intense and very self-involved.

As we adopt a more spiritual approach, however, we can develop a willful self-awareness which mitigates this, together with a rock-solid integrity that others can feel. At the spiritual level, this placement nourishes our creativity, our adaptability, and our resourcefulness with the life-giving properties of Haumea.

Danish writer, Hans Christian Anderson, is an example. His 'magic of being' inspired numerous generations. His fables of morality were translated into more than a hundred languages, more than any book other than the Bible. And, exemplifying the self-involvement of this House, he also wrote three autobiographies.

As we deepen our contact with Source, we learn to trust our gut instincts and develop a soulful confidence in our work. At this level, the life energy is pouring through us, and we can nourish others with it and may have the ability to foster psychic unity.

Like New Zealander Faye Blake-Cossar, who runs an astrology school in Amsterdam. Her master's dissertation offers a *"life cycle model for organizational development"* and her work focuses on making clients feel safe while applying her extensive training in Inner Child Integration Therapy.

Second House

With Haumea in the 2nd House, we can bring about a material rejuvenation, both in our own lives and in the world around us. We have the psychic power to manifest what we want in the real world when we open to Source and believe in ourselves.

At the personal planet consciousness level, we may have a bit of a bulldozer approach to our security needs and to our sensual pleasures, which may be successful in the short term, but things like bullying are not sustainable practices for a healthy life, nor is relying on non-paid volunteers, fans, or devotees for support. With this placement we need to ensure that we are giving as much as we are receiving, on both the material and the psychic levels, and that we remain faithful to our values.

As we develop a more spiritual approach, we likely have a deep appreciation of our sensual experience and of nature, and we understand the humanizing and social function of art. Because the 2nd House is about cultivation and Haumea is about fostering and fertility this is a very creative and generative placement.

Like Mae West, who wrote most of her material and became an icon of sexual power and femininity.

She was so faithful to her values of free creative and sexual expression that she was prosecuted for moral charges because her first Broadway play, *Sex*, depicted homosexuality. She bailed her cast out, but she chose to stay in jail herself to garner the publicity. We see the generative power of Haumea in this house in her status as the 2nd highest paid person in the U.S. at the height of her career.

As we deepen our contact with Source, this can bring a bountiful process of renewal into our lives which provides us with everything we need, and our sense of self-worth can also enjoy a constant state of renewal. At this level, we understand that psychic energy underpins everything in the physical world, and we can transcend the material desires of our ego.

Like revered Indian spiritual teacher, Nisargadatta Maharaj, whose teachings centred on the development of spiritual insight, understanding the illusory nature of the world, and finding liberation from suffering. His core message was that by recognizing and abiding in the eternal consciousness within, individuals could find true peace, freedom, and spiritual growth. He taught that identifying with the body and its desires was a hindrance to spiritual growth. Instead, he advocated for a shift in consciousness, recognizing oneself as the unchanging witness of all experiences, including the aging and decay of the physical body.

Third House

The renewal in the 3rd House is in our ideas, our communications, and our immediate environment.

Haumea is always searching for spiritual answers and in this House her curiosity infuses all our communications, if we can see the forest for the trees.

At the personal planet level, because this house talks about the lower mind, we may get lost in the trees, lost in the detail, and feel insecure in these contacts. And we may make up for this by demanding attention, or by making claims of martyrdom and sacrifice to secure attention.

As we develop a more spiritual approach there is likely a renewal process occurring in our thinking patterns which keeps them fresh and relevant and gives us the insight to see the divinity of human beings and the oneness of existence.

Like Erica Jong, who wrote *Fear of Flying*, which was controversial for its depiction of female sexuality, female liberation, and women's search for personal and emotional fulfillment outside of traditional roles and expectations. Her work catalyzed the development of second-wave feminism, fighting for reproductive rights and gender equality in the workplace, and against domestic violence and sexual harassment. She was married four times, embodying Haumea's ability to be reborn.

As we deepen our contact with Source, an unshakeable personal inner knowing emerges. Haumea's ability to reconstruct, redefine, and transform, especially regarding consciousness, is strengthened with this placement.

Like American musician, Van Morrison, who Rolling Stone magazine commented had *"the striking imagination of a consciousness that is visionary in the strongest sense of the word".*[10] He describes himself as a Christian Mystic and has investigated various religions, which serve as inspiration for his music.

Fourth House

The 4th House is the base of our consciousness, the sacred ground in which our consciousness is rooted, and with Haumea here we have a psychic connection to the oneness of humanity embedded within that consciousness.

At the personal planet level, however, this house shows the karmic baggage we brought with us into this life. And Haumea's placement here might make us a little too self-centered and a little too invested in getting our way so that we adopt a forceful approach. This house talks about instinctive behavior and Haumea is about opening doors within us, so our level of consciousness is crucial in seeing and evaluating those doors.

Indian born author Salman Rushdie has this placement. His work primarily deals with connections, disruptions, and migrations between Eastern and Western civilizations. His book *The Satanic Verses* generated debate in the Muslim world and provoked a backlash. The Supreme Leader of Iran, issued a religious decree, calling for his death. As a result, for many years he was forced to go into hiding and adopt a reclusive lifestyle, confined in the sacred space of his 4th House for his own safety.

As we develop a more spiritual approach, we can bring the spiritual wealth and rejuvenation of Haumea into our home and our inner emotional security. For those who believe in reincarnation, the 4th House gives us clues to our karmic lesson for this lifetime and with Haumea here the lesson is to reconnect with the psychic unity of humanity across time and space, to feel the oneness of existence.

Margaret Atwood has this placement. Her written works encompass themes such as gender and identity, religion and myth, the power of language, and climate change. Her famous sci-fi book, *The Handmaid's Tale,* explores the interdependence of the sexes in a futuristic dystopian world, causing the reader to question the usury nature of our relationships and move beyond them into embodying psychic unity.

As we deepen our contact with Source, we create a sacred space where we can base our consciousness. This base is a fertile sacred ground where we are always able to find nourishment for our higher consciousness. And our higher consciousness can always find the companionship of like-hearted souls.

Fifth House

The 5th House is all about us being ourselves and enjoying it, and with Haumea here we will likely be very creative in this process. With this placement, our joy will have a regenerative effect, both on ourselves and others.

At the personal planet level of consciousness, however, we may come on too strong in our love affairs, our creative self-expression, and our parenting. There is a risk of being overly dramatic and attention-seeking as a cover for our lack of real psychic connection. And this is the House of risk-taking, so we must be careful not to fill any lack of connection with others with hollow pleasures like gambling.

As we develop a more spiritual approach, we can learn to bring a spirit of play into our romantic affairs, our creativity, and our parenting, and to take the risks necessary to grow in these areas.

Like Philip K. Dick, whose fiction explored philosophical and social questions such as the nature of reality, perception, human nature, and identity. Embodying Haumea, he was married 5 times. Later in his life, following a series of mystical experiences, his work moved into the realms of theology and metaphysics.

Then, as we deepen our contact with Source, we gain a passionate understanding of the humanizing and social functions of art. At this level, the fostering ability and fertility of Haumea gives us a rich bounty of joy and love as the creative medium of our work.

Centering in love, Elisabeth Kubler-Ross, Swiss psychiatrist and author, is noted for her work in renewing our relationship to dying and death. Her belief in the continuity of life spirit through the experience of death enabled her to assist more than 20,000 people with their passage into an afterlife.

Sixth House

With Haumea in the 6th House of routine tasks and duties, every moment can be alive with spirit and in touch with the 'magic of being'. With this placement we have a magic touch which can breathe life into anything we turn our hand to, and particularly to the services we provide.

At the personal planet level of consciousness, however, we may not be aware of our gifts, and worry about our lack of meaningful connection could manifest in our lives as anxiety disorders. We have to be mindful not to play the hypochondriac or be attention-seeking to compensate.

This House also talks about our method of responding to everyday crises and, at this level, we may ride roughshod over people because of the urgency of our immediate demand. As we develop a more spiritual approach, Haumea gives us the willfulness to seek a strong psychic connection in each moment and the regenerative strength required in moments of crisis.

We see this in Farida, Queen of Egypt, who liberated women in Egyptian culture from their secluded role as mothers, to become participants in society. She did this by taking a public role as queen in her marriage, which also freed the other royal women from the seclusion of the harem. She later gave up the status of queen in order to divorce her husband and gain her personal freedom.

As we deepen our contact with Source, Haumea gives us the courage to see the divinity of human beings and the oneness of existence in every moment. At this level, we have an ability to reach out into the psychic soil around us and connect with both a larger wisdom and an unshakeable personal inner knowing.

Like Reinhold Ebertin, considered the founder of Cosmobiology, which holds that cosmic energies influence biological processes on Earth. This influence is evidenced by the Moon's impact on our waters. His work in this branch of astrology integrates psychology, medicine, sociology, and biology into an understanding of the rhythms of our daily lives.

Seventh House

This is the House of one-to-one relationships and with Haumea here our search for spirit is answered through our relationships. 7th House relationships are about cooperation and sharing, and they generally serve some functional purpose in the larger social community.

At the personal planet level of consciousness, however, we may experience quarrels and separation in our relationships if we are not tuning in to our partner. The lack of respect implied by our insensitivity can breed open enemies and lawsuits.

Like American filmmaker, Francis Ford Coppola, who had a rollercoaster career which forced him into bankruptcy three times in ten years as a result of bad investments of his early film profits. His iconic movie *"The Godfather"* nevertheless had a defining effect on modern culture. He was initially reluctant to direct it until he focused on the deeper themes of family and capitalism in America.

As we develop a more spiritual approach, we can engage in diplomacy which opens doors for us and others. Haumea's renewal comes both through a reconnection with our inner fountain of youth and with the collective psyche through our one-to-one relationships.

Like Jane Fonda, who has undergone a variety of reinventions in her life, including actor, exercise guru, feminist, political activist, author, businesswoman, and wife to a number of famous men. The title of her autobiography encapsulates her regenerative power: *Prime Time: Love, Health, Sex, Fitness, Friendship, Spirit – making the most of all of your life.*

As we deepen our contact with Source, we can reach a state of psychic equilibrium and enjoy rock solid integrity in our contracts and all official matters. At this level, we are able to connect with souls who can play important roles in our lives, psychically nourishing us, and them, as we find a new way of living together.

Eighth House

The 8th House rules the processes and things by which we transform and become more powerful, including through sexual interaction. So, this placement gives us a fountain of renewal to assist that empowerment.

At the personal planet level of consciousness, transformation usually requires some type of death, loss, or injury first. This is the House of karma, where we make personal sacrifices for the collective and at this level, we may be a bit of a drama queen, because Haumea likes to make claims of martyrdom and sacrifice to secure attention. Or we could abuse our psychic sensitivity by using other people's energy, taking advantage of non-paid volunteers, fans, or devotees.

However, as we develop a more spiritual approach, the regenerative nature of both the House and the planet work together to allow a flowing spring of spirit into our lives, keeping us in touch with the 'magic of being'.

Like Masaru Emoto, original thinker, Japanese artist, and author of *The Hidden Messages in Water*. His extensive research and photography of the frozen crystal form of water gave humanity striking visuals of how water is affected at a molecular level by what's around it.

Or like Jane Goodall, who is the world's leading expert in the social life of chimpanzees. She observed behaviors that we consider only human, like hugging, kissing, and even tickling, saying *"It isn't only human beings who have personality, who are capable of rational thought and emotions like joy and sorrow.*[11] In later years she founded Roots & Shoots, which brings together youth worldwide to work on environmental conservation and humanitarian issues.

As we deepen our contact with Source, we strengthen our occult ability, understanding the give and take required to maintain this flow. At this level, our sensitivity to the collective psychic energies can bring the clairvoyance to see how these energies will play out. We understand that the bountiful universe manifests through us when we are open to it. And, to enable this, we know that we have to leave our ego at the door and trust in the divine process.

Ninth House

Haumea is always searching for spiritual answers, and in the 9th House this is about the experiences we encounter when we search for the meaning of things. So, this placement sends us on a rich exploration of life.

At the personal planet level of consciousness, we could be locked into belief systems and experience head-on collisions with others who believe differently. Or we could feel insecure in intellectual areas, unable to make enough spiritual connection to make any sense out of our experience.

However, Haumea has an ability to reconstruct, redefine, and transform, especially regarding consciousness. As we develop a more spiritual approach, we are able to discover larger fields of social existence by synthesizing known data in a new way.

Like Patch Adams, who maintains that humor and joy are more important than any drug or therapy in the healing process. Recovering from psychological problems himself, he went back to school to become a doctor and set up the Gesundheit Institute, where he charges no fees, has no malpractice insurance, and lives with his patients in a country farm setting. At the institute, medicine is integrated with the performing arts, crafts, agriculture, nature, recreation, and social service.

As we deepen our contact with Source, this placement can bring an unshakeable personal inner knowing and put us in touch with the 'magic of being', accentuating Haumea's profound idealism and sense of freedom as the highest principle.

We see this in Icelandic musician Bjork's political support of liberation movements for Kosovo and Greenland. She also supports the individuality of young artists by helping them launch their careers. Her music is unique, and she and her fans share an alternative view of the universe.
"I think there's a spiritual element in everything. Walking down the street can be spiritual or it can be silly. It's up to the person. I can definitely say that making and listening to music are spiritual experiences for me."[12]

Tenth House

The 10th House encompasses the most public areas of our lives and the career that we develop, and with Haumea here we are in tune with society and are likely to be a reformer.

At the personal planet level of consciousness, however, we may have trouble connecting with this psychic oneness of society and so may come on too strong with our answer for others, alienating them and making our job harder.

But as we develop a more spiritual approach, we can open ourselves to this oneness that is all around us and draw strength from this, understanding the bigger picture. This house includes the social foundations of recognition for achievements and sense of duty to society. Haumea's placement here can bring the insight to see the divinity of human beings in all our social activities.

Like Scottish observational comedian, Billy Connolly, known for his crass use of language and reference to human bodily functions. His irreverence dissolves the social boundaries, uniting us as humans. *"I think it's time for people to get together, not split apart. The more people stay together, the happier they'll be."* [13]

As we deepen our contact with Source, we can embody this divinity and develop the spiritual wealth and rock-solid integrity that is the basis of the community power and prestige of this house. At this level, we feel the life energy and we can use this connection to enable social rejuvenation.

Like Italian educator Maria Montessori, who developed The Montessori Method which emphasizes the development of a child's own initiative and natural abilities through practical play. This method provided educators with a new understanding of child development that allows children to develop at their own pace.

Eleventh House

The psychic connection with Haumea in the 11th House is to our community, to the collective consciousness. With this placement we will gather a soul family and find a new way of living together with them. These people may be spread across the planet and may not be the obvious choice, but our connection will psychically nourish us and them.

At the personal planet level of consciousness, however, this can manifest as a lack of connection, because our sense of belonging is inward-looking. Or we may seek indiscriminate connection with friends or groups, or force a connection, because we are so desperate for belonging that we do not evaluate friends or groups appropriately.

As we develop a more spiritual approach, however, we can become more sensitive to this process and more aware of consciousness. At this level, the collective consciousness provides a rich field of opportunity for the profound idealism of Haumea, and we will actively seek out groups with like-minded views.

Leading Mexican artist, Frida Kahlo, exemplifies this profound idealism: *"I have a great restlessness about my paintings. Mainly because I want to make it useful to the revolutionary communist movement...until now I have managed simply an honest expression of my own self..."*[14]

Today she is regarded as an icon for the feminism movement, the LGBTQ+ community, and for Chicanos, the culture which embodies the in-between nature of cultural hybridity that is neither fully American nor Mexican.

As we deepen our contact with Source, the love and charity of this house combines with the spiritual wealth of Haumea, to enable us to redefine and transform the collective consciousness and foster the 'magic of being' in our lives and the lives of those around us.

Like Leonard Cohen, whose spirituality permeated all his work. He evolved from struggling writer to successful singer and songwriter and then became a Zen monk. Through his music we shared in his personal spiritual journey from an alienated space as a younger person to a strong connection with the magic of being alive. His music is known for being bittersweet yet gracefully expressing the dark night of the soul.

Twelfth House

This is the House of the collective unconscious and of spiritual realization and Haumea's placement here gives the potential for deep spiritual connection.

It is also the House of the subconscious, which is the hidden self that exists apart from our physical everyday reality. So, at the personal planet level of consciousness, we may not be in touch with this side of ourselves. As a result, we may inadvertently expose ourselves or have issues of privacy. Finding refuge, seclusion, or retreat may help us to reconnect with our inner 'magic of being'.

This is the house of spiritual realization and Haumea is

spiritual wealth. As we adopt a more spiritual approach, we can develop a psychic connection to the unconscious and, over time, this will enable luck and miracles in our life.

Like musician Arlo Guthrie, who bought an old church and made it into a charitable center that serves people of all religions through free lunches, aid for family farmers, and services for abused children and the elderly. As a renowned folk singer-songwriter he also holds a number of fundraising concerts each year that support families living with life-threatening illnesses. His personal exploration of spirituality includes Catholicism, Judaism, and Hinduism.

As we deepen our contact with Source, the supportive, fostering energies of Haumea combine with the healing, forgiveness, and peacefulness of this House to allow a deep spiritual connection with the oneness of existence.

Like Annie Besant who was deeply religious as a child and longed to serve humanity, which she did as president of the Theosophical Society for 25 years. In that role she fostered the young Jiddu Krishnamurti as the new spiritual avatar through her World Teacher Project. She had a great love of ritual and ceremony and wrote more than 300 books and pamphlets.

Chapter Six

Next, we develop our spirit consciousness with Quaoar, who, in myth, sings and dances the world into existence. Quaoar encourages us to find a practice to bring spirit into our physical lives. Song and dance are practices that call spirit into our lives, as are activities like meditation, yoga, bush walks, and even sport. Anything can be a practice to enrich our lives with spirit.

We can look at Quaoar as the higher octave of Jupiter. Both planets talk of expansion and of new possibilities, but where Jupiter expands through a mix of luck and a hunger for more, Quaoar repolarises Jupiter so we can see the new opportunities and deftly take the appropriate action to enable the expansion that is possible in each moment.

Where Jupiter is a sort of dumb luck, Quaoar turns each moment into a dynamic meditation, where we can see the opportunities and act on them in real time. So, Quaoar is like smart luck. Quaoar's energy is dynamic and present in the moment, working within our consensus reality, either just under the surface or just out in plain sight.

Quaoar is the song and dance we tell ourselves about our lives. Our unique song and dance is a spirit-story which underpins who we are. We want to be the centre of our story, so we tell ourselves and everyone who will listen about that drama, and we create and develop it in the process.

If we are experiencing this energy unconsciously, we won't be present in the moment, and we won't have all the information we need for our story to be successful. So instead, we snarl ourselves up in chaos through our lack of insight and thereby turn our lives into a soap opera. When our spirit-story is a soap opera, the drama is just as real, but without the connection to spirit that gives it meaning. Instead, it becomes just a series of moments which do not build or work together to create something greater.

At this level we could also be a doomsayer because we understand the power of these stories. Or we might try to control others through fear to get them to play along with our story. Our inability to access spirit might also give us a fear of change or of group involvement. Or we could find that our spirit is being suppressed by rules and regulations which are being imposed on us.

As we develop spiritually, however, we can learn to embrace a spirit of discovery, and to see life as a dynamic meditation. Quaoar's focus on practice is particularly valuable here, as we realize that anything can be a spiritual practice. We see that everything is valuable and that it can all be woven into the song and dance we are doing which makes sense out of the world for us.

At this level our connection to spirit enriches our lives, allowing us to be present in each moment, and revealing the possibilities available to create our reality. We begin to understand how we can push the limit of what is possible by working in harmony with others to create a richer spirit-story. We see how each creative act adds value to the whole and works together to reinforce our creative fervor.

At the spiritually evolved level, we experience the song and dance of spirit in everything, and we understand that we are part of a rich chorus of spirit which underpins the physical world. We see both the bigger spirit-story that humanity is telling, and the part we're playing in that story. This allows us to manifest spirit as required to bring order out of chaos and create harmony in our lives.

Beyond Gender

Quaoar is our first non-gendered deity. Quaoar is the creation deity of the Tongva people, indigenous to California. In today's pronoun rich environment, it is sobering to realise that we don't have one for someone who is non-gendered. This gives us an idea of the evolutionary spirit consciousness that Quaoar brings into our lives.

Quaoar Consciousness Challenges

Here are some exercises to help on-board spirit consciousness into your life. As always, they will be best focused in the area of your life represented by your Quaoar house position.

1. **Finding a practice.** If you don't have a practice to bring spirit into your life, or if you don't even understand what that means, try a few of the

popular options, like any yoga, any martial art, any meditation, all creative classes including singing and dancing, and even nature adventures, and see what you like.

2. **Do your own thing.** If you are allergic to group practices and so shy of classes, remember anything can be a spiritual practice, so if you don't fit into the popular practices, you are welcome to *'do your own thing'*. You probably are already. But remember practices are regular and the point is to bring spirit into matter, not just go through the motions.

3. **Giving thanks.** If you do have a practice to bring spirit into matter, congratulations. Reflect on the process involved in your practice. Consider how it nourishes you with spirit. And give thanks for the blessing.

4. **Write your personal spirit-story.** This is not your life story, but the story about the song and dance you are doing, and the influence that is having on the world. Putting this into words helps clarify it. Then notice how it develops over time.

5. **Consecrate your soap opera.** If your spirit-story is a soap opera, find a practice to bring spirit somewhere into that opera so it becomes creative and inspiring. Something in the opera can be turned into a practice... or you can just make the time for a yoga class... It doesn't take much to turn a soap opera into something deep and meaningful.

6. **Create something together.** If you don't usually collaborate, jump into any song, dance, or improvised theatre classes to practice this process.

Creating something together connects us to spirit. Choose an art form that you enjoy and let go of your inhibitions.

7. **Up level your luck.** Notice when opportunity knocks at your door, was it just blind luck? Or did you develop and foster that opportunity, and then act in the right place, at the right time?

8. **Saying yes to opportunity.** We have to see the opportunity and then act to embrace it, and both of these take practice. Improvised theatre classes are very good for teaching us to say yes to opportunity. When we're improvising with someone, we have to say yes to everything they offer, otherwise the magic of the story collapses. This is good practice for taking the Quaoar opportunities when we see them.

Quaoar in the Houses

First House

With Quaoar in the 1st House, we have a creative dynamic consciousness in our centre, one that can see the new opportunities and deftly take the appropriate action to enable the expansion that is possible in each moment. Planets in this house greatly influence our personality and how others perceive us and, with Quaoar here, we will have a strong sense of self.

At the unconscious level, however, this strong sense of self, together with the self-interest and ego-centredness of this house, can blind us to the bigger picture and to others' points of view, so that our wins are likely to come at a cost to others. We get so caught up in our own spirit story that we are insensitive to others.

As we develop spiritually, Quaoar's revealing energy in this house of self-awareness, encourages our consciousness growth. At this level, our spirit practice is likely to be dynamic, meditative and free of the need for faith. This allows us to connect with the divine and ground that spirit in reality at the same time. Through this practice, we come to understand the rich creative interplay which enables our growing consciousness.

Like American actor and writer, Steve Carell, who is known for his portrayal of characters who grow in consciousness through their personal struggles and through self-reflection. In his films like *Little Miss Sunshine,* and television series like, *The Office* and *Space Force,* he has a knack for blending humour with a genuine emotional core, creating characters who are flawed yet relatable.

At the spiritually evolved level, the resourcefulness and adaptability of this house, together with Quaoar's ability to bring order out of chaos and create harmony, enables us to constantly initiate consciousness growth in ourselves and others. At this level, our spirit-story becomes an inspiration to others, who join our practice and add to the rich chorus.

Like American psychic healer, Olga Worrall, who set up the New Life Clinic, a nondenominational religious service devoted to the healing of all physical and psychological illnesses. She believed the healing power came from God and made no claims about her own healing powers. She is the author of three biographies, *"The Gift Of Healing," "Explore Your Psychic World"* and *"Your Power To Heal"*, in which she explores the many facets of psychic experience from auras and astral travel to clairvoyance, possession, and dreams.

Second House

With Quaoar in the 2nd House, how we value ourselves will be at the centre of our cosmic dance of survival and security. As Quaoar is the higher octave of Jupiter, and this house talks about our potential for accumulation of wealth and material possessions, we can bring a smart-luck to dealing with the material world. With this placement, our body is our temple and when we honour that natural wisdom, we constantly carry the divine within us.

At the unconscious level, however, our focus is likely to be more on our sensual pleasure, and we may have a tendency to try to control others through fear. This house is about our ability to provide for ourselves, and at this level our ego may get in the way of our cosmic dance, bungling the transmutation of the chaos in our lives and turning it into a soap opera.

Like American religious leader, Louis Farrakhan, who is a rampant racist and inflammatory speaker. As the leader of the Nation of Islam, he has made controversial statements promoting fear, division, and animosity, particularly regarding race and religion. His rhetoric has been criticized for its potential to incite fear and distrust among different communities.

When we are on the spiritual path, however, our dynamic meditation empowers our generosity and our sense of self-worth increases as a result. Here we develop a more enlightened attitude towards possessions, valuing those essential to our practise. As we do this, we may find that our spirit story starts to generate resources.

At the spiritually evolved level, we can transmute spirit into matter, undistracted by passion or the promise of wealth. At this level, our spirit story talks of our own growth, and this inspires the growth of others. Here our ability to infuse spirit into our lives has material rewards both for us personally and for the world.

Like Dutch internationally known psychic, Jomanda, who is said to have restored sight and healed cancer. At the age of 28 she felt that she was clairvoyant and she began to practice healing. Four years later she performed her first miracle healing, then she started holding healing gatherings which drew large groups of people. For many years special trains were scheduled to take around 15,000 people a week, paying 10 Gilder a head, to her healing services.

Third House

Quaoar in the 3rd House of thinking patterns, urges us to question, clarify and reveal, and through a dynamic process to bring laws and harmony into our world. This is the house of ideas and communication and Quaoar's placement here indicates an ability to decondition ourselves from the confines of established intellectual concepts.

At the unconscious level however we might get tied up in details and small bits of information, or fall into doom-saying as a way of not getting disappointed. And we might not honour our physical needs and thereby block the link between spirit and our body: if we do, our spirit story is likely to speak of the results of this block.

Like renowned author and philosopher, Aldous Huxley, who explored dystopian and pessimistic themes in his works. His most famous novel, "Brave New World", portrays a future society characterized by totalitarian control, technological dominance, and the dehumanization of individuals.

When we are on the spiritual path, the connections and mental dexterity of this house provide a fertile ground for Quaoar's spirit of discovery. At this level we can learn to listen to the wisdom of our body, and honour the body as a temple through which we connect with spirit. This house is about classifying and examining information, and Quaoar's placement here gives an ability to bring both our creative and analytical sides to bear on this process.

At the spiritually evolved level, Quaoar's creativity and inspiration flowers through the intellectual stimulation of this house. As we embrace the generosity inherent in this placement, we may well make an inspirational contribution through writing and speaking.

Like Indian spiritual teacher and writer, Nirmala Srivastava, who was the founder and guru of Sahaja Yoga, which is practiced and taught for free in over 140 countries. During this meditation, practitioners experience a state of self-realization produced by kundalini awakening, a form of divine feminine energy located at the base of the spine. This is accompanied by the experience of thoughtless awareness or mental silence. Nirmala gave numerous public lectures, and interviews and never charged for her instruction.

Fourth House

With Quaoar in the 4th House, we can ground our reality and connect with our past through the creative practices we undertake in our home. This is the house of instinctive behaviour, and Quaoar here infuses our instinct with spirit. With this placement our spirit story will be rooted in our heritage and we may tell a multi-generational story.

At the unconscious level, the need for inner emotional security of this house might lead us to worship our physical body at the expense of our intellect, psyche or spirit. Or we might not look after our physical needs, and so block contact with spirit.

When we are on the spiritual path, we see our karmic lessons revealed in the dynamic process of our home life, which gives us the opportunity to process them. At this level, our spirit story, while rooted in our personal experience, can reach out into the world and resonate with others.

Like respected American astrologer, Robert Hand, who has been instrumental in blending traditional astrological principles with modern techniques. His work has expanded the scope of astrology, exploring its historical roots while incorporating a psychological and holistic approach. He seeks to help individuals understand themselves in relation to the larger world, promoting harmony by recognising the interconnectedness of human beings and the environment. He emphasises personal growth, self-reflection, and the achievement of harmony within oneself and the surrounding environment through astrological practices.

At this spiritually evolved level the cosmic song and dance we do on the sacred ground we create in our home will move our soul and bring harmony to our environment. Quaoar is a forward-looking spiritual energy, free of the influence of faith and submission, and in this house of roots and ancestors we are able to transmute this karma through a dynamic meditation process.

Like Indian saint, Anandamayi Ma, who used dynamic meditation practices in her home to help devotees release negative energy, cultivate introspection and awareness, and ultimately transmute their karmic lessons. Participants engaged in physical movements like dancing, waving their arms, or swaying their bodies rhythmically. By surrendering to the divine while embracing these rhythmic movements and chanting mantras, participants could connect with their inner selves and transform their karmic patterns.

Fifth House

Quaoar in the 5th House will bring a cosmic forward-looking dynamic to the process of being ourselves and enjoying it. The creativity and inspiration of Quaoar thrills to the creative self-expression of this House.

This is the house of love affairs and, at the unconscious level, we might worship the sexual experience and snarl ourselves up in a soap opera of affairs. There is also a danger of risk taking or gambling at this level, because we may be working from limited information.

When we are on the spiritual path, however, we learn to ask the right questions to get the information we need, and we can dare to take the spiritual risks required to grow in consciousness. At this level, we can participate in the cosmic dance of love, and learn to love selflessly.

Like American environmental activist and singer-songwriter John Denver, who was known to have a deep personal connection with nature and spirituality. He often expressed his reverence for the natural world and believed in the interconnectedness of all living beings. This connection to nature and his spiritual beliefs influenced his music and his advocacy for environmental and social causes. His songs have themes of love, peace, and harmony, and his music inspires listeners to connect with the beauty of nature, foster empathy, and embrace a sense of unity and understanding.

And at the spiritually evolved level, we have a dynamic unconditional love at the heart of the process of being ourselves. At this level, our spirit story will resonate with other people, attracting support for our work, and we might teach our passion.

Like American marine biologist, author and teacher, Rachel Carson, who had a deep passion for marine life and the environment which she shared with the world through her writings. Her book *Silent Spring* catalyzed the start of the environmental movement and her passion and dedication continue to inspire individuals to work towards a sustainable future. She believed that faith, respect for all life, a sense of awe and wonder, and deep feeling for the universe, were essential to studying and understanding nature, as well as finding solutions to modern problems.

Sixth House

With Quaoar in the 6th House of routine tasks and duties, we can approach these areas with a new magical perspective, which can strengthen our response to everyday crises. With this placement, skill development will be a dynamic ongoing process. Wellness and health are central to this house, and Quaoar's placement here can bring an intuitive connection to self, which gives us the ability to chart a wellness course through all challenges.

At the unconscious level, however, these magical new perspectives may elude us, so we are left living a soulless routine, unable to find a way of enlivening our lives with spirit. Our new perspectives may also turn out to be delusions that we either created or bought into. Or we may feel trapped in our job, or have issues with our physical ability to work.

When we are on the spiritual path, our daily routine becomes a dynamic meditation, which we can nurture through good diet and maintaining our vitality through regular practices. The caretaking of this house and the creative forward-looking energy of Quaoar work together at this level to serve and guide our spiritual path.

Like American folk singer and activist, Joan Baez, who advocates for maintaining vitality through practices such as mindfulness and making conscious choices about diet, exercise routines, and overall lifestyle. Mindfulness involves being fully present in the moment, aware of one's thoughts, emotions, and sensations, without judgment. By practicing mindfulness, she believes that we can cultivate a sense of peace, reduce stress, and enhance our overall mental well-being.

At the spiritually evolved level, Quaoar's placement here gives the courage, energy and connection to people, required to serve the divine in each moment. At this level, our spirit story resonates with the zeitgeist, and others will be drawn to join in the creative chorus.

Like the Indian spiritual master Sri Meher Baba, who dedicated his life to spreading a message of love, compassion, and unity as essential qualities for spiritual growth. He taught that unconditional love is the key to connecting with the divine within oneself and in others. He offered teachings on self-realization, inner transformation, and the inherent divinity within every individual.

Seventh House

With Quaoar in the 7th House we will be constantly seeking equilibrium in the cosmic dance of our one-to-one relationships. The relationships in this house are about cooperation and sharing, and this placement encourages a more engaged perspective which enables this interaction.

At the unconscious level, we are likely to be too self-involved, which will turn our lives into a soap opera of quarrels and separation, and potentially even open enemies, or lawsuits. These disruptions occur because we are not conscious enough of our partner and so we fail to factor their choreography into our dance, or their lyrics into our spirit-song.

Like celebrated American author, Scott Fitzgerald, who had a tumultuous relationship with his wife, Zelda. Their marriage was marked by quarrels, separations, and strains, which played a significant role in shaping the emotional depth and complexity of his characters. The couple were known for their extravagant lifestyle and for their partying, but they also experienced financial instability and emotional turmoil. The love, jealousy, and sense of unattainable desire that permeates his writing, can be traced back to this relationship.

Once we are on the spiritual path, however, we begin to see our relationships like a sacred dance that connects us with the divine, and we are likely to attract partners who share this view.

Then, at the spiritually evolved level, this placement brings a magical touch to all our relationships, and to the official and unofficial agreements and contracts that underpin them. We have an implicit understanding of where both sides stand and of the unfolding interactive dynamic.

Like American energy healer and mystic, Rosalyn Bruyere, who emphasizes the importance of understanding and harnessing the power of energy in relationships. One of her most well-known works is *"Wheels of Light: Chakras, Auras, and the Healing Energy of the Body."* She believes that by developing sensitivity to energy dynamics and utilizing various healing techniques, we can create and maintain more meaningful and fulfilling connections with others.

Eighth House

With Quaoar in the 8th House of transformation, we have the power to reshape our lives and the lives of our partners with whom we share joint resources. This is also the house of karma, debt and judgment, so we will be held to account for our actions, but Quaoar brings a forward-looking perspective which helps with this process. Sex is likely to be good at all levels with this placement.

At the unconscious level, however, we may be so caught up in the soap opera of our lives that turns it into a financial drama with the possibility of losses and bankruptcy, or problems with inheritances and taxes. At this level, our spirit story gets caught up in our mundane dramas.

Like well-known American psychic and author, Sylvia Browne, who faced criticism and lawsuits concerning her predictions. Critics argued that they were often vague and open to interpretation, lacking substantial evidence or proof of their validity. The inconsistencies or inaccuracies undermined her credibility with some people, and she faced lawsuits centred around allegations of false advertising, fraud, and deceptive practices.

Once we get on the spiritual path, the self-transformation potential and occult ability of this house provides our

Quaoar with a rich playground for growth. Quaoar urges us to question, construct, clarify and reveal and in this house Quaoar asks the deepest questions and reveals the biggest answers.

At the spiritually evolved level, we realise that body and spirit are one. At this level, we have a deep inner connection with the occult and are likely to be able to dynamically channel these energies. At this level, our spirit story becomes a chorus that others can resonate with, and participate in.

Like renowned Bulgarian artist, Christo, known for his large-scale environmental installations. His works often reflected a deep understanding and appreciation for the unity of body and spirit, and explored concepts of transcendence and the connection between art and spirituality. Through his installations, he challenged the boundaries between the physical and spiritual realms, creating a palpable sense of connection between the viewer, the artwork, and the surrounding environment. This immersive experience allowed viewers to move beyond their ordinary perception of space and engage with a more profound sense of existence.

Ninth House

With Quaoar in the 9th House, we experience our cosmic song and dance through a process of exploration in the world, and we might enable this by participating in higher education or by travelling. This is the house where we reach out and search for meaning, so this placement enhances our spirit practice and strengthens our spirit-story.

At the unconscious level, however, we could run into issues with the law or behave unethically because we are too caught up with our personal point of view to understand how others see it. This is the house of dreams, and it is our perspective that will make the difference between these manifesting in our lives as a personal soap opera, or as spiritual vision.

This is the house of big-picture thoughts, and once we get on the spiritual path, the philosophical interests, schools and belief systems here provide a wonderfully rich playground for our search for new perspectives.

This is exemplified by American psychotherapist, astrologer, lecturer, and teacher, Tracy Marks, who is the author of 15 books including *"The Astrology of Self Discovery."* With a Master's Degree in psycho-synthesis, she is acclaimed for her in-depth integration of psychological, spiritual and astrological concepts. She is skilled at leading dream work, women's empowerment, and the art of friendship groups.

At this spiritually evolved level, Quaoar's placement here enables us to weave together disparate threads and be playful with the sacred, so we come to a deep new understanding. We are able to synthesize known data and weave this into a new synthesis, a flowering of new thoughts and ideas.

Like Bulgarian philosopher and teacher, Omraam Aivanhov, who dedicated his life to exploring esoteric teachings and sharing wisdom on topics such as spirituality, personal development, and the transformation of humanity. He was known for his ability to make complex spiritual concepts accessible, often using humour and playfulness in his teachings.

Tenth House

With Quaoar in the 10th House, we will play a dynamic social role in the magical process of giving new form to chaos. We are able to manifest these new opportunities through our participation in society. We may well enjoy recreational activities like singing or dancing and, if we are creative, we could work in the performing arts.

At the unconscious level however, the responsibilities that come with this house could drain our energy and leave us exhausted. At this level, the more we 'try and sort it out', the more we are likely to snarl ourselves up in a vast soap opera, the cast of which will include everyone we know.

Yet once we get on the spiritual path, we learn to embrace a spirit of discovery in our social interactions and see the sacredness in each moment. At this level, we can allow a lightness or a playfulness, which enables a bringing together of people and energy, and gives an ability to weave them into a new togetherness.

Like South African anti-apartheid revolutionary and political leader, Nelson Mandela, who became the first black President of South Africa. Throughout his life, he worked tirelessly to promote equality and reconciliation among all South Africans. He played a crucial role in uniting the nation during a time of great division and strife, advocating for peace, forgiveness and understanding. His leadership and ability to bring people together have made him an iconic figure in the pursuit of unity and social justice.

At the spiritually evolved level, we learn to see life as a dynamic meditation, in which we can see the professional opportunities in the chaos that we find around us, and deftly take the appropriate action to enable the expansion that is possible. At this level, we find meaning in the challenges we face and our spirit story will have a rich social fabric.

Like renowned Chilean-American writer, Isabel Allende, who has written extensively on themes of love, loss, and the human spirit, weaving spiritual and metaphysical concepts into her storytelling. She believes in the power of resilience and finding meaning in difficult circumstances, and, facing personal and professional challenges herself, she has consistently found opportunities for growth and creativity by embracing the chaos of life.

Eleventh House

With Quaoar in the 11th House, our cosmic song and dance is about our search for connectedness, for belonging and for love. This is the house of self-realisation and Quaoar brings a magical dynamic to this process.

At the unconscious level, we could be susceptible to conspiracy theories or become involved with cults or organisations which present a different world view. At this level, our need for belonging may blind us to the agenda behind the groups that we are involved with, and this can open us to a form of brainwashing.

Quaoar in the 11th House wants freedom, but we have to understand what this means before we can find it. Once we get on the spiritual path, we begin to recognise it when we see it. At this level, we can enable the enormous self-realisation potential of this house and find the appropriate community of interest to support our growth.

Like British trade unionist and women's rights activist, Mary MacArthur, who fought for better working conditions for women and successfully organized various strikes and campaigns to improve labour rights. She understood that individual empowerment and self-realization could be achieved through finding and joining a community of like-minded individuals with shared goals. By working together, she was able to create a supportive network that fought for workers' rights and championed women's equality in the workplace.

Love is what enables the 11th House connectedness and at the spiritually evolved level, Quaoar's placement here can generate a fountain of love in our interactions with friends and social groups. Here the connectedness and networking of this house, work together with the dynamic meditation of Quaoar to expand the collective consciousness.

Like French-Swiss film director, screenwriter, and producer, Jean-Luc Godard, one of the most influential filmmakers of the 20th Century. His films, such as *"Breathless"* and *"Weekend,"* challenged traditional storytelling and societal norms, encouraging us to question established structures and ideologies while fostering a sense of love and connection among diverse groups of characters. His work is characterized by a desire to transcend traditional religious boundaries and find meaning and transcendence in our human experience, which encourages the viewer to rethink their understanding of the sacred and its role in society.

Twelfth House

With Quaoar in the 12th House of the collective unconscious, we inherently know that our body and our spirit are one, and we feel the pulse of the moment. This is the house of secrets and hidden enemies and Quaoar's revealing energy here, is likely to bring these to light.

At the unconscious level, however, we may be too self-involved to get a clear perspective of what these are, and we may slip into addictions, or snarl ourselves up in a soap opera involving institutions like hospitals, prisons, or government offices. At this level, we might deny the spiritual and compensate by indulging in the physical world.

When we are on the spiritual path, the healing and forgiveness of this house, and the 'wisdom of the body' of Quaoar, provide rich opportunities for the growth of our consciousness. At this level, we can use sacred bodywork to balance intellectual stress and the demands of objective consciousness, and we can draw on the unseen world for guidance.

Like Dutch parapsychologist and gifted healer, Gerard Croiset, who was known for his abilities in extrasensory perception and psychometry. He had the ability to perceive information through means other than the conventional senses, including telepathy, clairvoyance and precognition. He became well-known for his accuracy in providing specific details about missing persons, crime scenes, and other unsolved cases.

And at the spiritually evolved level, we can learn to manifest spirit in our lives and bring order out of the chaos in the collective unconscious, thereby creating harmony. With this placement, we feel the collective pulse, are in contact with the divine, and our spirit story will resonate with the zeitgeist.

Like French mystic, Marthe Robin, who, despite being paralyzed and bedridden for most of her life due to a severe illness, founded a spiritual community centred around prayer, meditation, and service to others. Her experiences and teachings emphasized the importance of surrendering oneself to God and finding meaning within suffering. She believed that by embracing our struggles and aligning our life with God's will, we can manifest spirit and bring harmony to the collective unconscious.

Chapter Seven

Through Makemake we develop a systems consciousness and learn to innovate. Makemake drives Spirit into our lives, opening us to the new richness of this sacred consciousness. When we are in tune with this consciousness, we understand that we are each a speck in the vast universe, and yet the spirit energies can flow into us and nourish us when we are devoted and in the natural rhythm.

Makemake encourages us to see ourselves as an organic whole. We are not just the sum of our disparate parts, we are living beings in which the parts work together to bring us to life. And he encourages us to look at our community in the same way and understand the role we are playing in the larger organic wholes, or teams, of which we are part. The first of these is our family, and then our school, our work, and all the other teams of which we are a member.

The members of a team work together. Through participation and understanding of the teamwork process, we learn how to be sensitive and tune in to our fellow team members. As we connect to others on an empathic level, we tune into collective consciousness and find a way to work together. When we come to see and understand how we are affected by our social context, we are able to be in the right place at the right time to play our part.

We can look at Makemake as the higher octave of Uranus, which is traditionally the higher octave of Mercury. Makemake gives Uranus's intuitive impulses meaning and context, which transforms our understanding of his unexpected ways, while Uranus's lateral web gives Mercury's detail an energetic network to organize and connect his information. All three planets are tricksters, and Makemake is a spiritual trickster who allows us to experiment with the area of life signified by his position in our chart.

Makemake is keen to learn. While he shares Mercury's curiosity, he is looking at the bigger picture as well as the detail. He talks about freedom, expansiveness, and keen vision, and he encourages us to develop a richer awareness by taking old ideas and playing with them experimentally to liberate their active components.

We know that Uranus brings us intuitive insights, and we have to honour them for the valuable insights that they are, and then act on them, or we risk our intuition manifesting in our lives in a more Saturnian way, so that we eventually get the lesson. With Makemake we need to embrace the rich culture that is created through all these insights. There is an inherent fractal structure in the rich detail of our lives, so that any part of the structure references all other parts.

Makemake reveals this structure, which is the model that we build of our world from Uranus's intuitive flashes. There is no 'real' world, there are just phenomena which we interpret based on our experience. A new-born baby sees colour and hears sounds, but they have no Makemake framework to make any sense of it. This model grows over time as we learn to interpret the phenomena around us. Then we react, based on that interpretation, and so shape our reality through those responses.

So we create our world by how we perceive it and interact with it. Until now, this has largely been an unconscious process, but as we embrace our systems consciousness, we begin to understand the creative power of our personal view of reality. This is the power that 'great minds' have to shape the consensus view.

However, when we are at inner planet consciousness, we likely have a more limited, short-term view, which encourages us to cut corners where we see that we can. At this level, Makemake can encourage us to be reckless, and our lack of respect for traditional ideas can lead us to engage in double talk and be manipulative with our communication.

We might lose sight of the bigger picture and, as a result, we may not want to play by the rules or cooperate with others. We could indulge in practices such as backbiting and rivalry, which undermine our own position. Or we could try to hog the limelight, rather than humbly play our part, thus sabotaging the collective success.

We could also take flight to avoid the consequences of our actions or develop an ability to hide in plain sight as a coping skill. Makemake enables us to understand the context of each moment and, at this level, we may use that understanding to blend into the background like a chameleon: like those characters in television ads whose clothes are patterned like the wallpaper, we are only seen when we move.

As we develop a more spiritual approach, we develop the devotional focus to understand the rich tapestry of our lives held in each moment. Through Makemake's fractal nature, we also see the cosmos in each of those moments. The cosmos is the biggest system that we are part of, and, at this level, our systems consciousness becomes a cosmic consciousness.

The more we develop spiritually, the more Makemake's cosmic consciousness cuts through our personal feelings to reveal the bigger perspective necessary to transform our understanding of ourselves. As we do, our contact with the bountifulness of cosmic consciousness allows us to joyfully participate in our lives, because we feel the profoundness in each experience.

At this level, we are able to alchemically break down existing ideas into their component parts and then put them back together in new configurations. We understand the context behind the ideas, and this enables us to be playful in this process. As we formulate our new ideas, we become inspired to manifest them by winnowing them down into usable applications.

And at the spiritually evolved level, we can see the big picture and integrate this with our personal devotional focus with such depth that it will likely be called genius. As we deepen our cosmic consciousness, we experience the world as an organic whole, which allows us to participate in that whole as fully as possible.

At this level, we know that we'll get best results when we embrace our dharma with an unflinching gaze and a fierce grace that leaves no detail out. Everything that we discover becomes a valuable, creative resource for our growth. We are able to see things as they are and have the power to take action in the face of any eventuality.

Embracing the New Richness

We need to embrace the rich culture that is created through our insights, and we have to trust in our reality model and use it to engage with the world, rather than use it as camouflage to keep us safe from attention. It works both ways, but the more we engage with the world, the more opportunity we have to refine our model and develop it.

We have to get in our model and drive it around in order to continually update it based on our new experiences. The more we expand and test our dataset, the better our model becomes and the more useful it is in charting our way forward. Playfulness is a way of removing the fear of failure in this process. There is no failure because all the data is valuable. It's only a failure if we don't integrate the experience, causing the 'bad' outcome to happen again.

However our reality model is not a toy car we can play with. We are cultivating an ineffable, infinitely complex understanding which unconsciously informs our choices in each moment. So, the way we get in it and drive it around is to simply face up to the challenges we encounter each day.

Makemake Consciousness Challenges

Here are some consciousness exercises to help on-board this energy into your life. They will be best focused in the area of your life represented by your Makemake house position.

1. **Objectify your worldview.** Find a piece of art, a short text, or an object which epitomises your worldview and place this somewhere you see it regularly. Then notice how your appreciation of it changes over time. Update your objectification as needed.

2. **Practice devotion.** Find an area of strong interest to you and give yourself permission to devote as much time as you can to your interest. This can be in any area of life, but it is best focused in your Makemake house. To avoid getting lost in your obsession, make sure you do the basics of looking after yourself and taking care of your personal reality at the same time.

3. **Play with your reality model.** Our understanding of the world is reinforced by the patterns in our lives. If you feel constrained, or uninspired by your model, try going somewhere new. Put yourself in a new situation to see how your understanding develops in that context. And remember, a playful attitude is the best way to approach this new divine consciousness.

4. **Work with your team.** Reflect on the organic wholes that you are part of. Understand the role you play in each of them and also the roles your teammates are playing. Then be as sensitive as you

can to your teammates to find the best way to work together.

5. **Change your wallpaper clothing.** If you are using your Makemake to stay safe by blending in, and you want to change that, try standing out in a small way to start with. Change one thing about your wallpaper-clothing so you are more visible in some way and learn from the results.

6. **Shift your perspective.** If you are already using your Makemake to get out and engage with the world, try a 'vow of silence' challenge for a couple of days to gain a different perspective. Silence doesn't mean you don't engage, just that you do it non-verbally. Studies show that 45% of communication is emotional tone and 50% is physical expression, so you can still use both those and also write notes if you need to. Choose a good couple of days when you have the space, and it might help to wear a little card saying: 'I am observing silence'.

Makemake in the Houses

First House

With Makemake in the 1st House of self, we will be clever and quick-witted and have the devotional focus to understand the rich tapestry that each moment holds. This is also the house of how others see us, and with this placement we will likely be thought of as insightful, and can act as an inspiration to others.

At the unconscious level, however, this is the house of our self-interest and our ego, so our systems consciousness could encourage us to get ahead by being verbally manipulative, or engaging in double talk and diversion of facts, or simply not playing by the rules. This is also the house of our defence mechanisms, and with this placement we could take flight to avoid consequences or hide as a coping skill.

For example, Oliver North was a National Security Council staff member in the USA during the Iran–Contra affair, which was a political scandal involving the illegal sale of weapons to Iran to encourage the release of American hostages then held in Lebanon. North diverted the proceeds from these arms sales to support the Contra rebel groups in Nicaragua. He was convicted of aiding and abetting in the obstruction of Congress, accepting an illegal gratuity, and altering and destroying documents.

However when we are on the spiritual path, we can develop a deep self-awareness. At this level we understand the complexity of groups and cultures and also how they function as an organic whole. We are therefore able to play a facilitating role in these organisations and cultures.

Consider Gertrude Stein, who was an American writer and icon of modernism. She moved to Paris at age 29, where she held weekly salons with the likes of Picasso, Hemingway, Wilder, Matisse, and F. Scott Fitzgerald in attendance. These gatherings brought together the talent and ideas that would define modern literature and art. Stein described her writing style, not as stream of consciousness, but as an "excess of consciousness".

At the spiritually evolved level, we embody our world view, and we can joyfully participate in our lives. At this level, we are vital and resourceful, and our cosmic consciousness enables us to understand the rich tapestry that each moment holds, so we can maximise our engagement and impact.

Second House

With Makemake in the 2nd House of resources, we can bring a devotional focus to the process of gaining and spending our money which permits extreme talent in this area, however this can come at the expense of neglecting other things. This is the house of security needs and Makemake can give us the fast footwork and the ability to learn from experience that is required to achieve a comfortable life.

Yet, at the unconscious level, the desire for sensual pleasures might get in the way of the drive for money and possessions. We might behave recklessly and in a self-serving manner, looking after ourselves, rather than playing by the rules or cooperating with others. At this level, our systems consciousness enables us to cut corners where we see that we can.

However, when we are on the spiritual path, we can approach the material world with less attachment and with a greater sense of joyful participation. Through this, we build a deeper and more realistic understanding of how it all works. At this level, Makemake enriches our values, ensuring we are in the right place at the right time.

Like Marie Curie who, along with her husband, conducted pioneering research on radioactivity, a term she coined. They were awarded the Nobel Prize for Physics when she was 36. She was the first woman to receive a Nobel. She so valued the rich material world that she went on to discover two new elements - polonium and radium - for which she earned a second Nobel Prize, this time for Chemistry.

And, at the spiritually evolved level, we learn to value and cultivate both the rich spiritual world and the rich material world around us. At this level, our cosmic consciousness drives spirit into our lives and opens us to see the bigger picture.

Like Richard Tarnas, a U.S. cultural historian, astrologer, and teacher, who did his doctoral dissertation on *'LSD psychotherapy, psychoanalysis, and spiritual rebirth'*. He is well known for his third book *Cosmos and Psyche: Intimations of a New World View,* in which he shows that the major events of Western cultural history correlate consistently and meaningfully with the transiting squares and oppositions of the outer planets.

Third House

With Makemake in the 3rd House of ideas and communication, we will be clever, quick-witted and verbally self-assured. This is the house of our thinking patterns and Makemake, being a spiritual trickster, allows us to experiment with these.

At the unconscious level, however, we might get lost in the details and the small bits of information, or be verbally manipulative, engaging in double talk and simply not being straight with the facts. At this level, we could also be prone to gossip about others, or engage in backbiting and rivalry. And we may take flight to avoid the consequences of our actions or develop an ability to hide in plain sight as a coping skill.

Then, when we are on the spiritual path, we learn to make the right connections for our growth and communicate effectively with each of them. At this level, we will be articulate and able to foster the give and take necessary for effective teamwork. And we may be able to simplify the infinite complexity we experience into a practical framework that others can use.

Like Elizabeth Kübler-Ross, a Swiss-born psychiatrist whose early experiences inspired her to dedicate her life to healing. In her first book, *On Death and Dying,* she pioneered psychological counselling to the dying through her now famous Five Stages of Grief - denial, anger, bargaining, depression, and acceptance. And she went on to become the author of 24 books published in 41 languages.

At the spiritually evolved level, our cosmic consciousness will be able to invoke insight and inspire others. At this level, we can facilitate group integration, by enabling the group to act as an organic whole. This insight into the culture in all its rich detail, gives us the ability to be in the right place at the right time and understand how best to maximise our growth and influence.

Like Jiddu Krishnamurti, who was discovered as a 14 year old in India by the Theosophical Society and groomed to be their next World Teacher. However, at age 34, he closed the order saying: *"Truth is a pathless land... I want to do a certain thing in the world and I am going to do it with unwavering concentration: to set man free. I desire to free him from all cages, from all fears, and not to found religions, new sects, nor to establish new theories and new philosophies."*[15] Yet he went on to tour the world and give talks until his death at age 91.

Fourth House

Makemake in the 4th House will open us to see the bigger personal picture and enable us to draw spirit into a sacred space in our home. With this placement, we are able to nurture our roots and our psychological foundation through an infusion of spirit. We understand how our inner psychology connects with the organic whole of who we are.

Yet at the unconscious level, the conflicts, fears and dreams involved in family issues are likely to play a large part in our world. We may get caught up in the drama, and not fully understand the consequences of our actions. If we feel that our inner emotional security is challenged, we may stop playing by the rules or cooperating with others, or we could be verbally deceptive or manipulative, or try to hide as a coping skill.

Like Amy Grossberg, a U.S. teenager who hid her pregnancy from her family. Even after she and her boyfriend secretly birthed their baby boy in a motel, she refused to accept his existence. They put the child in a plastic bag and left him in a dumpster where he was later found and diagnosed as having been a live, healthy birth. He had died from multiple skull fractures and apparently from having been shaken. Grossberg blamed her boyfriend, pleaded for leniency and told the judge, *"I want to help others. I want to make a difference."*

On the other hand, when we are on the spiritual path, we can find the devotional focus to understand the rich tapestry of karmic lessons that each moment holds. At this level, we have the cosmic consciousness to know that we are each a speck in the vast universe, but the spirit energies can find us and nourish us when we are devoted and in the natural rhythm.

And, at the spiritually evolved level, our complex understanding of the way the world works will gain the support of others, and we may become a master of a spiritual system that can connect with others on a soul level.

Like David Cochrane, a U.S. astrologer whose empirical research in astrology and consultations with thousands of clients has formed the basis for his development of Vibrational Astrology. *"Astrology, like literature and art, enhances one's perspective and is edifying to the soul... This is why astrology has persisted through the ages. People do not cling to astrology because they are superstitious, gullible, and stupid. They cling to astrology for the same reason they cling to literature, art, and music; they lift the soul."*

Fifth House

With Makemake in the 5th House, we will be able to enjoy experimenting creatively with our lives, taking the risks required to be ourselves in each moment. This is the house of creative self-expression and we are able to bring a devotional focus which enables us to develop extreme talent in this work, but this can come at the expense of neglecting other areas.

This is also the house of love affairs and, at the unconscious level, we might engage in double talk to facilitate our sexual relationships, and be manipulative with our communication about our love. At this level, we could also get involved in speculation or gambling, acting recklessly by putting short term advantage ahead of long-term gain.

Like French exotic dancer and spy, Mata Hari. During the First World War her neutral status as a Dutch citizen enabled her to cross borders when the love of her life, a young Russian soldier, was wounded. However, this came at the cost of becoming a spy for France. She was tasked with seducing the Crown Prince of Germany and, to gain access, she offered him intelligence. As a result, she was accused of being a double agent for Germany, was arrested by the French and tried for treason, then executed by firing squad.

When we are on the spiritual path, however, we can learn to joyfully participate in the creative risks of being alive, and to work as part of a team to achieve common aspirations. This joyful participation will lead to a richer awareness and we might teach our passion.

At the spiritually evolved level, we are open to spirit and able to love unconditionally. At this level, we can see the bigger picture and this cosmic consciousness enables us to invoke insight and inspiration through our quick-witted, creative work.

Like American astrologer Philip Sedgwick, who is known for his Deep Space and Whole Sky astrology. A self-proclaimed researcher by nature, he compiled a Galactic Ephemeris of more than 8,700 deep space objects. He has taught and presented internationally, and he uses comedy to communicate his heavenly messages. His books include *The Astrology of Transcendence* and *The Astrology of Deep Space*.

Sixth House

With Makemake in the 6th House, we will likely be clever and quick-witted as we go about our daily routine or do our job. This is the house of health and physical sickness, and we have the ability to listen to ourselves and foster our wellness through appropriate responses in each moment. We can also use fast footwork in our response to everyday crises and are able to join with others and work as a team to achieve common aspirations.

At the unconscious level, however, we might not see the advantage in teamwork, and we may engage in double talk, saying one thing while we do another. Or we could play fast and loose with the facts to gain short term advantage, essentially not playing by the rules or cooperating with others.

Like conservative U.S. media personality, Sean Hannity, who, until recently, was the highest paid Fox News anchor. He is known for promoting "deep state" conspiracy theories. According to The Washington Post, Hannity *"repeatedly embraces storylines that prove to be inaccurate"* and takes positions on a range of topics that change over time.

When we are on the spiritual path, we understand that the spirit energies can find us and nourish us, if we are devoted and in tune with ourselves. At this level, we learn to call the nourishment of spirit into our lives through the services we perform.

Like former US Secretary of State, Condoleezza Rice, who grew up in Alabama while the U.S. South was still racially segregated, yet completed her Ph.D. in political science by the age of 26. She became the first female African-American U.S. Secretary of State and the first woman to serve as national security advisor. She said of this time: *"To have a chance to serve my country as the nation's chief diplomat at a time of peril and consequence, that was enough."*[16]

At the spiritually evolved level, we can embrace the divine in the rich tapestry of each moment of our lives, and we know that we'll get best results when we do it with an unflinching gaze and fierce grace that leaves no detail out. At this level, everything becomes a valuable, creative resource for our growth, and our cosmic consciousness enables us to develop a devotional focus in our service to others.

Seventh House

With Makemake in the 7th House, our relationships bring us freedom, expansiveness, and connection to spirit, opening us to see the bigger picture. With this placement, we are articulate with those closest to us, and able to see through the legalese of contracts and all things official.

At the unconscious level, however, we could fall into backbiting and rivalry, quarrelling with our partners, and engaging in double talk and manipulation to maintain our relationships. At this level, we could also take flight to avoid the consequence of our actions or develop enemies and become involved in lawsuits through our reckless and self-serving approach.

In the extreme, we can see Adolf Hitler, whose policies and promotion of the Holocaust inflicted human suffering on an unprecedented scale. Of the five women he has been romantically connected to, three were roughly two decades younger than he, and only one lived a long life and died of natural causes. Two died by suicide, a third died of complications from her attempted suicide, and the fourth also attempted suicide.

Yet when we are on the spiritual path, we begin to understand the give and take required for our relationships to work, and we can develop the ability to work together as a team. At this level, our cosmic consciousness enables us to understand that each relationship we have is perfect for our growth, and we learn to be diplomatic and cooperative with our significant others.

At the spiritually evolved level, we can develop cooperative partnerships and joyfully participate in them, conscious of the organic whole that is created by being together. At this level, we have the devotional focus to appreciate the rich tapestry created by our network of relationships as we foster each of them.

Like the iconic talk show host Oprah Winfrey, who has garnered countless awards stemming from the reputation she built through her one-to-one relationships on *The Oprah Winfrey Show*. She is known as an empathic and authentic communicator who is able to draw out the rich tapestry of people's life stories, and make a strong connection with her audience. She has said: *"I have church with myself: I believe in the God force that lives inside all of us, and once you tap into that, you can do anything."*[17]

Eighth House

With Makemake in the 8th House, we have the systems consciousness to understand how we interact with the collective energies in our lives to form an organic whole. This is the house of karma and this placement helps us feel the complex intermingling of karmic energies in each moment, tuning us into the bigger picture.

At the unconscious level, however, we might act in a reckless and self-serving way with our joint resources, which can lead to losses, debts, or bankruptcy. At this level, we might have to make personal sacrifices to facilitate the regeneration necessary in our lives.

Like American entrepreneur Martha Stewart who rose from a modest background to become the first female self-made billionaire. She was known as a shrewd, competitive, and even ruthless businesswoman. However, she committed insider trading and was subsequently indicted by a grand jury on nine counts, including charges of securities fraud and obstruction of justice.

However, when we are on the spiritual path, our cosmic consciousness gives us the courage to experiment with the occult and discover the rich tapestry of self-transformation possible in each moment. This is also the house of commitments of all kinds and, at this level, we will be competitive and engage in best practice.

And, at the spiritually evolved level, we understand the cycle of death and rebirth. At this level, we can see the big picture and can integrate this with our personal devotional focus at such a deep level, that we may have a clairvoyance about how things are playing out in our lives and what is to come.

Like American astrologer Steven Forrest, one of the founders of Evolutionary Astrology, which embraces paradigms and methodologies that specifically measure the growth of the soul from life to life. Asked about free will versus fate, he said, *"I am personally confident that we humans are capable of changing ourselves, capable of evolution. None of us is limited to a 'nature' that is cast in stone by the positions of the planets. As we change ourselves, we make different choices and thus create different futures."*[18]

Ninth House

With Makemake in the 9th House, we are interested in big thoughts and big ideas and we can experiment with them to gain a richer awareness. We are able to bring a devotional yet playful, focus to this work, through which we can develop our cosmic consciousness and uncover the real meaning of things.

At the unconscious level, however, religion might substitute for our individual research, providing the answers so we don't have to do the work ourselves. Our spiritual laziness could also lead us to develop questionable ethics and morals, engaging in double talk and playing loosely with the facts to support our version of reality.

Like Julian Assange, an Australian hacker and activist who founded WikiLeaks. To avoid extradition on charges of sexual assault in Sweden, and conspiracy to commit computer intrusion in the U.S., he was given asylum for 7 years in the Ecuadorian Embassy in London. And, after a dispute with the embassy, he has since been held in a British prison for 4 years while his U.S. extradition charges are disputed.

In an interview with the Sydney Morning Herald in 2010 he said: *"The sense of perspective that interaction with multiple cultures gives you I find to be extremely valuable, because it allows you to see the structure of a country with greater clarity, and gives you a sense of mental independence. You're not swept up in the triviutalities of a nation. You can concentrate on the serious matters."*[19]

When we are on the spiritual path, however, this placement is rich in the philosophies and the learning opportunities that we need for our growth. At this level, we might be a bit of a spiritual trickster, with an experimental, practice-based approach to our search for spiritual meaning.

And, at the spiritually evolved level, we can gain understanding and wisdom through our joyful participation in the process of taking old ideas and playing with them experimentally to liberate the active components.

Like astrologer Eleanor Bach, unsung champion of the asteroids, whose 1973 book *Ephemerides of the Asteroids* put Ceres, Pallas, Juno, and Vesta on the astrological map. She paved the way for Demetra George's work representing *"new voices of the dormant feminine, recently activated and now demanding power, recognition, justice and equality in our society."*[20]

Tenth House

With Makemake in the 10th House, we will be communicative and self-assured in our professional work and have a deep understanding of the culture or nation with which we are involved. We may take on a public speaking role or get involved with training people or groups to operate in a social context.

At the unconscious level, however, we could act in a reckless and self-serving way in our profession or take flight to avoid the consequence of our professional actions. Our systems consciousness enables us to exploit the holes in our social system. At this level, we could also develop the ability to hide in plain sight as a coping skill or try to overcompensate by hogging the limelight.

Like U.S. industrialist John D Rockefeller Sr, who came from humble beginnings. He had such a keen eye for the long-term role that petroleum would play in post-Civil War USA that his company Standard Oil monopolized 90% of the market until it was disbanded by a Supreme Court ruling. Rockefeller is still widely known as the richest person in modern history and the United States' first billionaire.

When we are on the spiritual path, we can become socially responsible and find the devotional focus to understand the rich tapestry of our lives that each moment holds. We develop the cosmic consciousness to see what we can do to help society develop.

Like U.S. First Lady Betty Ford, who, as a result of her own journey with substance abuse and addictions to pain medicine and alcohol, established the Betty Ford Centre, thus bringing greater national awareness and acceptance to this closeted issue. By speaking candidly, she helped to destigmatize this and other hot topics such as women's rights, gay rights, equal pay, abortion, breast cancer awareness, sex, drugs, and the AIDS crisis.

Then, at the spiritually evolved level, we can invoke insight and inspiration in others, and may become well known and receive honours through this work. At this level, we can see the organic whole of the culture and also how we can most effectively play our part in it.

Eleventh House

With Makemake in the 11th House, we will be receptive to collective forces and seek out groups that can help us expand our systems consciousness. This is the house of our hopes and goals, and with this placement we can see the big picture and integrate this with our personal devotional focus so we can play our part in the collective.

At the unconscious level, however, our need to belong might lead us to get involved with groups that purport to be one thing and are actually something else. At this level, our ambition could also lead us to act recklessly and in a self-serving way in the groups that we are part of, not playing by the rules or cooperating with others.

Like U.S. financier Bernie Madoff, who was found guilty of having defrauded about 37,000 investors across 136 countries of billions of dollars over his forty-year career. As the mastermind of the largest Ponzi scheme in history, at the age of seventy he was sentenced to 150 years in prison and died there twelve years later.

When we are on the spiritual path, we can adopt a more charitable attitude and joyfully participate in the self-realization that is possible in this house. At this level, the give and take of teamwork in the groups to which we belong, brings a richer awareness, and opens us to see the bigger picture.

Like renowned artist and civil rights activist, Maya Angelou, who had a difficult childhood. She was raped at age 8 by her stepfather, who was later killed for his crime, causing her to go mute for 5 years, as she feared the immense power of her words. When her first memoir, I Know Why the Caged Bird Sings, was published, it was a watershed not only for her, but for women and for Black people. Although known for her 7 autobiographies that bend the genre, her life itself was her art.

At the spiritually evolved level, we can adopt a loving approach to our community, drawing spirit into our lives in the process. At this level, our cosmic consciousness can play with the collective consciousness to liberate the active components and extend collective awareness.

Twelfth House

With Makemake in the 12th House, we are involved in a deep investigation of our subconscious and also of the collective unconscious of the culture in which we live. With this placement, we can bring a devotional focus to our habit patterns that come from the past, recognising how they underpin the rich tapestry of each moment.

This is the house of the self that we don't show to others, and, at the unconscious level, we might double down on this by developing an ability to hide in plain sight as a coping skill. At this level, we could also become involved with secret relationships and engage in double lives.

Like Arnold Schwarzenegger, who is widely known as a Hollywood actor and, in later years, became governor of California. However, his 25-year marriage to Maria Shriver of the Kennedy family ended when he admitted to fathering a child with their long-time housemaid. The affair was kept secret for thirteen years until the housekeeper brought her son to work one day.

When we are on the spiritual path, however, we can practice self-sacrifice and forgiveness, enabling us to release our karmic debts and heal our subconscious wounds. At this level, we value seclusion as a means to connect with the divine, and we understand that we are each a speck in the vast universe, yet the spirit energies can find us and nourish us, if we are devoted and in the natural rhythm.

At the spiritually evolved level, our cosmic consciousness enables us to always be in the right place at the right time. At this level, we are connected to the divine in each moment and may experience revelations or miracles.

Like social reformer and feminist, Annie Besant, who championed women's rights and workers' rights. She was among the first women to promote birth control, for which she was arrested. Annie also advocated freedom of thought and was a prolific speaker and writer. When she was forty-three, she became head of the Theosophical Society and remained president until her death 26 years later. In this role, she was instrumental in discovering and grooming Jiddu Krishnamurti to be the next "World Teacher."

GONGGONG

Chapter Eight

Gonggong awakens within us an empathic consciousness which is both benevolent and wise. Empathic consciousness gives us the ability to understand and share the feelings and emotions of others, enabling us to connect with them on a more profound level and promoting compassion and understanding in our interactions. The heightened emotional intelligence of empathic consciousness is an essential component of building positive and meaningful relationships.

When we can lift ourselves out of our personal emotions, Gonggong enables us to "walk a mile in another person's shoes". When we can feel inside those we are interacting with and understand the game from their side, we have the opportunity to motivate them and shift their energy through our responses. So, we can think of Gonggong at this highest level as an empathic wizard.

He encourages us to participate in the marketplace of life, to joyfully work with the give and take of energy within our community which is essential for our survival. When we do this, Gonggong brings good luck, prosperity, and abundance. Through our sensitivity to the energy flows, we are able to position ourselves or our product to maximize our potential, and, by participating in this social interplay, we can become wealthy and successful.

At the inner planet level of consciousness, however, he encourages us to indulge in the power of our personal emotions, rather than lift ourselves out of them to empathize with others. At this level, we are likely to be ambitious and cruel in our interactions, and we might behave in a selfish or zealous way and indulge in fits of rage. The release of the rage feels so good and so justified, that we can easily indulge in the emotion, reinforcing a feedback loop that grows until it is overwhelming, which just leaves us feeling drained and ashamed of our outburst.

Or we could be working against ourselves by striving for closeness, while at the same time using distance and aloofness to keep ourselves safe. We might be lost in detail. Or be jealous of others, putting ourselves at the mercy of their emotional pressure. At this level, unwilling to accept the shame of failure, we may choose to bring everything down with us when we feel we are losing.

Our assumptions are crucial here, as it is the incorrect ones that will lead to problems. When we assume something, we fail to continually check it against feedback from our environment, so it can become out of date, or our assumption might also be wrong to start with, but we've never really stopped to check.

At this level, we may feel overwhelmed with the emotions in our lives, and unable to see a clear path forward out of the morass of our personal feelings. At these points the key is not to indulge in this overwhelm, but rather to allow ourselves to float to the surface and then rise above it.

We need to channel the energies in our lives in order to avoid overwhelm. Damming doesn't work, because everything just builds up behind the dam. So, we need to practice channeling emotions or energy when we are feeling overwhelmed. This is not a withdrawal-and-refresh process, but a participation-and-refresh process, where we find an application for the emotion or energy in real time.

We tend to feel at these times that by lifting ourselves above the overwhelm, we are not dealing with important lessons. However, the reverse is true, the divine work is to let go of the base emotions so we can be sensitive to the emotional community in which we are nestled and open to the empathic support of others.

As we develop a more spiritual approach, we begin to understand that we live in a symbiotic relationship with the 'others' in our lives, and that we can pool our energy to achieve collective aims. We learn to calibrate our emotional pressure to meet the needs in each moment, and we develop the ability to channel our emotions and mold our psychic space to improve our productivity.

At this level, our empathic consciousness gives us access to a great wisdom, which can enable our enlightenment. We understand that the more we respect and harmonize with the energy flows in our lives, the better the future looks. We develop the ability to catalyze transformation and change in our own lives, and the lives of those around us. Ongoing renewal is facilitated by learning to nurture the cyclical nature of life.

And, at the spiritually evolved level, this becomes a cosmic nurturing of the emotional and psychic bonds between us. Our empathic consciousness is able to magically stir the energies in our lives to foster connections, endowering us with the ability to manage any emotional flow or overflow that may arise as a result.

At this level, we can channel spiritual, psychic, and emotional energies, and we can have watershed moments that generate floods of insight. These can put us in touch with the spirit world, or with cosmic wisdom, enabling us to irrigate and water the garden of our lives.

Social Interplay

Gonggong at the unconscious level can be very emotionally indulgent. What's happening for us is so important, and we are so lost in our own experience, that nothing else matters. As a result, we can be cruel and heartless to those around us.

Emotions are our instinctive response to the events in our lives. They motivate us to respond immediately, short circuiting our process of conscious assessment so we can survive in those dangerous moments when we must make split-second decisions. Unfortunately, this makes our emotions a largely unconscious process and, because of this, we often feel we are at the mercy of our emotions. We feel that our emotions take us over and that we are no longer in conscious control.

And we also like to wallow in emotions, because they are strong, and powerful, and are more real to us than much of the rest of our experience. If we are not conscious of them however, our emotions will run our lives, motivated by all the stuff that we have repressed and not dealt with. But we can become conscious of our emotional process and direct our emotions, just as we do our thoughts.

This enables us to lift our energy out of an indulgent space and into a co-operative interchange with others. Gonggong flowers and becomes an empathic wizard when we take full advantage of the social opportunities, lifting our own and other's energies through social interplay.

Gonggong Consciousness Challenges

Here are some consciousness exercises to help on-board this energy into your life. They will be best focused in the area of your life represented by your Gonggong house position.

1. **Enjoy social interplay.** No matter how much we try to be an island unto ourselves, social interplay is the lifeblood of survival. Consider some of your recent social interactions. You have the power to change your life by changing how you respond in any one of those interactions. Identify an area of your social interplay that you enjoy and would like to develop and play with it. Try different responses and follow your bliss.

2. **Do a personal stocktake.** Ask yourself: *"What am I bringing to the marketplace of life?"* It might be something you do, or it could be you, yourself. Consider how you interface this with the social environment and make adjustments as needed to enhance this interplay.

3. **Breaking out in rage.** Next time this happens, try deescalating straight away. This is hard because it feels so justified, and yet there is no good outcome

from rage. Suck it up, and then lift your energy out of your own emotions and open to empathy with the others involved. Learn to get over yourself.

4. **Deal with overwhelm.** Practice channeling emotions or energy when you're feeling overwhelmed, rather than blocking them or withdrawing from the intensity of them. Channeling is a participation-and-refresh process, where we find an application for the emotion or energy in real time.

5. **Empathy through mimicry.** Choose a busy pedestrian area and watch how people are holding their bodies as they walk. They are all unique. Then hop in a couple of meters behind someone whose movement you like and imitate their walk. Try to get the same feeling in your body as you sense in theirs. This is Gonggong sensing. Notice how different the world feels when you walk in someone else's shoes. Don't worry, no-one will notice and, if they do, just break off and walk on normally.

6. **Excite the baby.** Here's a party game to learn how to lift other people's energy from the inside. When it's your turn, sit cradling an imaginary baby and build a relationship with it through your facial expressions and sounds, just as you would a normal baby... (No words, to get you away from thinking. And the key to this is for the baby to be as real as possible in your imagination) ... Then start to excite the baby with your expressions and noises. And when you feel the baby loved that last thing you did, lift your head up and give the same noise and

expression directly to your friends... (To avoid being distracted by the vulnerability you might feel at the emotional reactions of your friends, go straight back to the baby) ... Find a new sound and expression and keep going, exciting the baby and then the audience in different ways. Let it happen naturally from the imaginary emotional contact, don't try to plan it.

Gonggong in the Houses

First House

With Gonggong in the 1st House we will have an enthusiasm for life and an ability to empathize with others and work collaboratively with them. We have a compassionate outlook and emotional reserves we can call on when needed, understanding that everything is a process and that through our involvement we will discover what we need to do next.

At the personal planet consciousness level, however, we might be coming from an ego centered, selfish understanding of these abilities and use them to manipulate others emotionally. We might find ourselves having fits of rage when we are frustrated, likely followed by a sense of shame for our outburst. We can energize ourselves emotionally this way but must learn not to get carried away, and to channel that energy constructively.

As we develop a more spiritual approach, we can learn to channel and calibrate our emotions to meet the needs in each moment, and to mold our psychic space to improve our productivity. At this level, we understand the process of dealing with karma and creating dharma, so we can make an uncompromising assessment of our spiritual state, which catalyzes our growth.

Like British nurse, Edith Cavell, who became known for helping soldiers from both sides during World War I, regardless of their nationality, and for aiding in their escape from German-occupied Belgium. Her commitment to her duty and higher principles eventually led to her arrest and execution by the German authorities. However her work exemplifies her empathic consciousness, and her unwavering dedication and sacrifice exemplify the uncompromising assessment of her spiritual conviction.

And at the spiritually evolved level, we can nurture the emotional and psychic bonds between us and have an ability to manage any flow or overflow in our interchanges. At this level, we can lift the collective vibe, exerting a benevolent and wise influence on collective consciousness. We understand that the more we harmonize with the energies in our lives, the better the future looks.

Like highly respected Tibetan Buddhist teacher and spiritual leader, Rinpoche Shamar, whose teachings focused on meditation, mindfulness, compassion, and understanding the nature of the mind. He founded the Infinite Compassion Foundation, an international aid organization committed to the rights of minorities and girls in the Himalayan region, through the construction of schools, the provision of medical care, and by promoting animal protection.

Second House

With Gonggong in the 2nd House, we are resourceful and can always find a way to get ourselves, or our goods, ready for sale and into the marketplace. This is the house of how we gain and spend our money and, with Gonggong here, we are likely do this in a collaborative or interactive way.

At the personal planet consciousness level, however, we could be ambitious and cruel with this placement, using others to achieve our selfish goals. Or we might be jealous of others and either full of fury as a result, or else find ourselves at the mercy of their emotional pressure. At this level, our vanity may make us unwilling to accept shame, so we choose to bring the whole temple down with us when we feel we are losing.

However, as we develop a more spiritual approach towards wealth and material possessions, we are better able to play the market to our advantage and find the sweet spot where we or our products or activities, can best be appreciated.

Like Indian spiritual leader and guru, Sri Sathya Sai Baba, who gained a significant following due to his teachings on love, compassion, and self-realization. He established a variety of charitable institutions and projects that aimed to serve society in various areas, such as education, healthcare, and social welfare. His ability to attract millions of followers and gain financial support for his projects, shows a spiritual understanding of market dynamics.

At the spiritually evolved level, we have the empathic consciousness to channel the psychic and emotional flow of energies in our lives, so they are constructively employed. At this level, we understand that we reap what we sow, and the more we contribute, the more we benefit personally and gain materially.

Like well-known American-British astrologer and author, Liz Greene, one of the most highly respected astrologers of the 20th century. She has written extensively on the psychological and spiritual dimensions of astrology. Her work often delves into the intricate connections between astrology, psychology, and spirituality, highlighting the ways in which we can understand and work with the psychic and emotional energies in our lives in a constructive and transformative manner.

Third House

With Gonggong in the 3rd House, we are enthusiastic and love to brainstorm ideas and be involved in conversations. With this placement, our empathic consciousness can see through the normal patterns of life, and this insight morphs our perspective to a higher level of consciousness.

At the personal planet level, however, we might find ourselves lost in detail, or find that we might not have accurately assessed our own needs before speaking. Or we might air our 'laundry', our emotions, or our possessions in public, and then deny responsibility and rationalize the response we get as someone else's fault or be bitter about our lot in life. At this level, our assumptions are crucial in determining how successful we are in our interactions.

As we develop a more spiritual approach, we can release our assumptions and develop the ability to channel our empathic contact and mold our psychic communication to maximize the opportunity in each moment. At this level, we can develop a leadership role in these areas through the trial and error of experiential analysis.

Like American spiritual teacher and author, Analee Skarin, who practiced mindfulness and cultivated a deep empathic understanding of herself and others. She was able to empathically connect with clients, while receiving intuitive guidance from higher realms of consciousness.

Through these channels, she was able to access profound wisdom and divine messages that positively impacted her clients. Her goal was to maximize each moment's potential to bring guidance and spiritual transformation.

Then, at the spiritually evolved level, we have a magical ability to create watershed moments where one psychic release empowers downstream activity. At this level, we are a spiritual wizard, able to stir the psychic waters to foster connections and bring illumination.

Like well-known Israeli psychic and illusionist, Uri Geller, who gained fame for his telepathic and psychokinetic abilities, such as bending spoons with his mind. He captivated audiences with these demonstrations, igniting curiosity about psychic phenomena, and stirring the psychic waters to create a sense of wonder and intrigue about the mysteries of the human mind. By pushing the limits of what we perceive as possible, he encouraged us to question our own beliefs and consider our own potential for untapped psychic and intuitive abilities.

Fourth House

With Gonggong in the 4th House, we are likely to have a busy home, full of interaction. It will be a place where people come together, drawn by our empathic consciousness. With this placement, we understand that we reap what we sow, and we value the process of working with our karma and creating our dharma.

At the personal planet level of consciousness, however, we might not feel secure in this process and may be competitive, or socially conscious to a fault. Or we could be jealous of others, particularly those in our home, and either full of fury as a result, or at the mercy of emotional pressure. At this level, we could be working against ourselves, striving for closeness, while at the same time using distance and aloofness to keep ourselves safe.

As we develop a more spiritual approach, we can embrace our natural compassion and sense of fairness and learn to bring spirit into our empathic contact. At this level, we can strengthen the base of our consciousness through an uncompromising assessment of our spiritual state.

Like American author, Richard Bach, who is known for his spiritual and philosophical writing, particularly in his book *Jonathan Livingston Seagull*. By exploring themes of self-discovery, love, and the pursuit of meaning and purpose, his work encourages us to connect with our inner self and strive for personal growth and fulfillment. He promotes empathy and understanding as tools to foster connections and create a more compassionate and harmonious world.

At the spiritually evolved level, we have the empathic consciousness to nurture the emotional and psychic bonds between the people around us. At this level, we can create a sacred space for ourselves and for others to contribute through social interplay.

Like the French mystic, Saint Bernadette, most well-known for her visions of the Virgin Mary. In these visions, she received messages of faith, hope, and healing, which brought comfort, inspiration, and a sense of connection to those who heard them. Numerous accounts of healing and miracles were also attributed to her intercession. The shared experience of witnessing these visions and messages created a sacred space for social interplay and deepened the emotional and psychic bonds among believers.

Fifth House

With Gonggong in the 5th House, we are enthusiastic participants in recreational and creative activities, and in affairs of the heart. With this placement, we enjoy being ourselves, and we want to be involved in the world. How we are involved will show what we need to do to bring our talents, skills, and wares to the marketplace.

At the personal planet level of consciousness, however, we might be a little too self-involved to pay enough attention to the others in our lives and so gain a reputation as a user. Or we could be working against ourselves, striving for closeness, while at the same time using distance and aloofness to keep ourselves safe. At this level, we could also be jealous of others and so, at the mercy of our emotions. Or we might get overwhelmed with our love and carried away with our passion and then experience regret and shame for our excess.

As we develop a more spiritual approach, we can embrace our compassionate nature and learn to calibrate our emotional responses to meet the needs in each moment. At this level, our creative endeavors flourish, and we are able to catalyze and nourish the emotional and psychic energies of those we love.

Like renowned American hypnotist and author, Dolores Cannon, who believed in the power of love, understanding, and empathy to bring about healing and transformation. By facilitating an exploration of past lives and connecting clients with their higher selves, she encouraged them to tap into their own inner wisdom and guidance. Through this process they were able to uncover and release emotional blocks, traumas, and limiting beliefs, allowing them to experience emotional healing and spiritual growth.

At the spiritually evolved level, we can develop a more unconditional approach to love, where we can maximize our empathic contact with others and, through this, the symbiotic potential of all our interactions. At this level, we are sensitive to the emotional community in which we are nestled and can nurture the empathic support within that community.

Like renowned American author, John Steinbeck, who often focused on social issues in his books, by portraying the struggles of the marginalized and disadvantaged with compassion and empathy. Through his storytelling, he aimed to shed light on human suffering and promote understanding and unity among people. His works promote empathy, compassion, and a sense of shared responsibility for the well-being of all members of society.

Sixth House

With Gonggong in the 6th House, we can nourish our well-being in each moment and cultivate a healthy lifestyle. With this placement, we might find ourselves working in areas that involve interacting with people and understanding them from the inside. This is the house of how we respond to everyday crises, and, with Gonggong here, we can call on deep emotional and psychic reserves.

However, at the personal planet consciousness level, we might have a bit of a 'bull in a china-shop' approach, thrashing around and ratcheting up the emotional pressure to achieve our goals. Or we might refuse to accept responsibility for our position, and project our problems onto others.

As we adopt a more spiritual approach, our empathic consciousness develops, which enables us to channel our emotions and mold our psychic space to improve our productivity. At this level, we can develop our compassionate understanding of the people we meet in our daily routine, or our job, and learn to assist them emotionally and psychically.

Like British writer and novelist Aldous Huxley, whose compassionate understanding of people is evident in his depiction of the complexities of human emotions and relationships. In his writing, he explores themes of love, suffering, alienation, and the quest for meaning. This encourages his readers to question conventional belief systems and explore alternative perspectives. It prompts them to contemplate their own spiritual journey, leading to personal growth and an expanded understanding of themselves and the world around them.

At the spiritually evolved level, we can create watershed moments where one psychic release empowers downstream activity and changes the course of history. At this level, we are an emotional and psychic wizard, able to stir the waters in our daily contacts, to foster spiritual connections.

Like American astrologer, Kelley Hunter, who integrates myth and astrology in her work, fostering strong emotional and psychic connections. By exploring how the planetary positions in a birth chart correspond to archetypal patterns and themes found in mythology, she invites her students and clients to engage with their charts in a more profound and meaningful way. Combining the language of astrology, with the rich symbolism of myth, she creates a space for emotional resonance, self-reflection, and personal growth.

Seventh House

With Gonggong in the 7th House, we will have a deep empathic connection in our one-to-one relationships. With this placement, being involved with our significant others is most important, and we see relationships as a process in which our interactions show us what we need to do next.

Yet, at the personal planet consciousness level, we could be shy of this involvement or comply with our partner and likely be codependent as a result. Or we might experience overwhelming emotional interactions in our close relationships, which make us wary of them. At this level, we can also be selfish and irascible, experiencing fits of rage when crossed, followed by a sense of shame.

As we adopt a more spiritual approach, however, we can develop a deep empathy and compassion for our partners. At this level, we learn to calibrate our emotional pressure to meet the needs of each person, in each moment.

Like renowned American dancer and choreographer, Martha Graham, whose innovative approach to modern dance placed a strong emphasis on emotional expression and human experiences. She worked collaboratively with her dancers, valuing their artistic contributions and providing a safe space for them to express themselves authentically. Her approach fostered an environment of trust and support, enabling her partners to explore their own emotional depths and deliver powerful performances.

Finally, at the spiritually evolved level, we understand the value of social interplay and can maximize the opportunity that is presented in each of our interactions. At this level, we can stir the waters in our relationships to foster consciousness growth, and our view of relationships may promote the growth of consciousness on a broader scale.

Like American screenwriter and producer, Gene Roddenberry, who created the *Star Trek* series. Gene's vision of the future presented a utopian society where humanity had overcome its differences and was working towards a greater collective consciousness. The characters and storylines in *Star Trek* pushed boundaries and challenged societal norms, encouraging viewers to question and re-examine their own beliefs and values. His work promoted empathy, understanding, and personal evolution, ultimately fostering consciousness growth.

Eighth House

With Gonggong in the 8th House, we can stir the psychic waters and we have a talent for bartering and for completing the deal. With this placement, we inherently understand the karmic and dharmic process, knowing that we reap what we sow.

At the personal planet consciousness level, however, we might sense the emotional and psychic power available, but not have the awareness to know how to direct it.

At this level, we could be zealous and pushy about our demands on joint resources or in our attitudes towards the deep mysteries of life, which is likely to arouse resistance in others. Or we might sacrifice ourselves for a fervent cause, and then feel resentful of our need to do this.

As we develop a more spiritual approach, we can learn to be uncompromising in our assessment of our spiritual state and to channel guidance to assist our growth. At this level, we have the empathic consciousness to understand the process of change occurring in each moment and can participate in, and catalyze, this process.

Like Indian spiritual teacher, Nisargadatta Maharaj, whose teachings emphasized the non-dual nature of reality as the path to self-realization. He encouraged his followers to question their beliefs, release attachments, and transcend the limitations of the ego. Through his direct and uncompromising style, he guided seekers towards the understanding of their true nature and the ultimate reality beyond the illusion of the self.

And, at the spiritually evolved level, we have a wizard's ability to nurture the emotional and psychic energies in our lives, and in the lives of those around us. At this level, we have a transforming relationship with spirituality, able to step up our own spiritual energy, and that of those close to us.

Like renowned American astrologer and author, Jodie Forrest, who has written books on astrology, spiritual growth, and personal transformation. She sees astrology as a tool for personal growth and spiritual development and her work often explores the deeper meanings and symbolism behind astrological signatures. She delves into the psychological and spiritual dimensions of astrology, helping individuals tap into their inner selves, understand their life's purpose, and navigate transformative processes.

Ninth House

With Gonggong in the 9th House, we seek out the deep spiritual meaning in the experiences we have, and we can become a spiritual wizard. With this placement, we have an ability to learn by immersing ourselves in experiences and absorbing the knowledge generated through our encounters. As a result, we likely enjoy studying and also traveling to new places and meeting new people.

However, at the personal planet level of consciousness, we may experience a lack of fairness in these encounters and so feel bitter about our lot in life. Or we might be blind to the part we play in these encounters and act in a selfish or a zealous way which alienates those with whom we're interacting. At this level, unwilling to accept shame, we may choose to bring the whole temple down with us when we feel we are losing.

As we develop a more spiritual approach, we strengthen our compassion, and understand that, the more we give, the more we get back in return. We have a strong sense of fairness and can grow through an uncompromising analysis of our own experience. At this level, we are sensitive to the subtle energies that underpin our everyday reality and may be able to channel divine guidance.

Like Brazilian author and medium, Zibia Gasparetto, who had the ability to channel the spirits of deceased authors and receive their messages which she transcribed and published as books. One of her most popular is the *Violetas na Janela* series, which were dictated by her spiritual guide. These books share spiritual teachings, insights into the afterlife, and personal experiences from the perspective of spiritual entities.

And, at the spiritually evolved level, we will have a deep spiritual understanding and can motivate and arouse this spiritual passion in others. At this level, we have the empathic consciousness to connect with the divine and channel guidance which fosters development of our higher selves.

Like American spiritual intuitive, trance channeler, and author, Kevin Ryerson, known for his ability to enter a trance state and allow spiritual entities to communicate through him. During these sessions, he has channeled a wide range of beings, including historical figures, spiritual guides, and even beings from other dimensions. Through his work, he aims to assist others to connect with their higher selves and find their own unique spiritual truth.

Tenth House

With Gonggong in the 10th House, we will be ambitious to get ourselves and our products out on display in society where we can be appreciated. With this placement, we love being part of a bigger social enterprise and we can take full advantage of our social opportunities to profit from the ventures we are involved in.

At the personal planet level of consciousness, however, we might be too selfish and competitive to build the relationships we need to succeed, or we could be cruel to our workmates. Or we might be vain about our place in society and socially conscious to a fault, unable to rock the boat in any meaningful way. At this level, we may also experience fits of rage and lash out when we feel we are losing, choosing to destroy everything if we can't have it ourselves.

As we adopt a more spiritual approach and deepen our compassion for the people in our professional lives, we can develop strong team-building skills. At this level, we have the empathic consciousness to motivate and channel the energies of our coworkers, to create a more organic and fair system that empowers each member.

Like American statesman and Founding Father, Thomas Jefferson, who believed in the inherent rights of individuals to life, liberty, and the pursuit of happiness. He advocated for these rights and worked towards their protection through his writings, including in the Declaration of Independence. His strong leadership and team-building skills were evident in the political alliances he built to champion individual rights, religious freedom, education, and the abolition of slavery.

At the spiritually evolved level, we revel in social interplay, understanding the benefit of working together and the multiplying effect on our energy when we do. At this level, we can nurture the emotional and psychic bonds in our professional lives, stepping up the potential of all members and lifting the spiritual energy in our social environment.

Like Indian spiritual leader and humanitarian, Mata Amritanandamayi, who teaches selfless service as a spiritual practice, inspiring her followers to engage in volunteer work and charitable activities. She believes that by coming together for service projects, we connect with one another, transcend our own self-centeredness, and experience the transformative power of collective actions toward a common cause. By creating spaces for people to connect, learn, and practice together, she encourages the development of a global spiritual community that works collectively to uplift the spiritual energy of society.

Eleventh House

With Gonggong in the 11th House, we will be an enthusiastic participant in social groups and in consciousness raising activities. We have an ability to feel the pulse of a group and can step this energy up to a higher spiritual level through our interaction with the members.

At the personal planet level of consciousness, however, we might be striving for closeness while using distance and aloofness as a defense. Or we could be zealous about our ideals and prepared to make sacrifices for them, but then feel resentful of this need, harboring rage as a result. Or we might air our emotions and dirty laundry in public and then feel a sense of shame for our outburst.

As we adopt a more spiritual approach, we deepen our compassion and learn to nurture the emotional and psychic bonds in our community through our participation. At this level, we develop the ability to read the room and play to our strengths, as well as to the strengths of the others in our group.

Like British comedian Tracey Ullman, who is known for her ability to create unique and memorable characters that often satirize societal norms and behaviours. These characters cleverly highlight the absurdities and contradictions present in society, encouraging viewers to reflect on their own beliefs and biases, and consider alternative perspectives. By addressing the emotional and psychic bonds between people in her comedy, she provokes thought, encourages dialogue, and promotes a more inclusive and empathetic society.

At the spiritually evolved level, we can remain centered in the melee of the market, able to parse the energy of those around us through our participation. At this level, we have the empathic consciousness to inspire and motivate members of our group to work at a higher spiritual level and bring them together to focus this energy where it has the most potential.

Like Hungarian Canadian spiritual teacher, Swami Sivarama, who is a leader in the Hare Krishna movement. He delivers inspiring teachings that highlight the importance of growth on both personal and collective levels. His teachings tap into people's aspirations and help them envision their own potential, igniting their motivation to take action. He is known for fostering a sense of unity and community among his followers, encouraging them to come together, support each other, and work collaboratively towards the common goal of spiritual growth and service.

Twelfth House

With Gonggong in the 12th House, we have a deeply compassionate nature, understanding that we reap what we sow. With this placement we know that we must work with our karma and create our dharma, so we will be enthusiastic participants in the zeitgeist. We learn that our assumptions are crucial, as the incorrect ones can lead to problems interfacing with the world around us.

This is particularly true at the personal planet level of consciousness, where we might have trouble connecting in any meaningful way with our world and might not be able to find our place in it. This could make us compliant to the will of another or of the system or leave us feeling marked as a target and bitter about our lot in life. Or we could play people off each other as a way of keeping ourselves safe and creating a smokescreen of drama.

As we develop a more spiritual approach, however, we learn to be uncompromising in our assessment of our own spiritual state and that of those around us. At this level, our empathic consciousness can nurture and motivate those in our world, simply by being ourselves in their company.

Like Peruvian American anthropologist, mystic, and author, Carlos Castaneda, known for his books about the teachings of Don Juan, a Yaqui Indian shaman. In these books, he explores awareness, personal power, and the importance of living in the present moment. By delving into shamanic practices, spiritual journeys, and encounters with extraordinary experiences, he inspires readers to explore their own consciousness and search for deeper meaning in their lives.

And, at the spiritually evolved level, we can call on deep spiritual reserves. We have an ability to stir the waters to foster connections, and the capacity to manage any psychic or emotional flow that may result from this.

Like Spanish mystic, writer, and reformer, Saint Teresa of Avila, who was renowned for her deep spirituality, mystical experiences, and writings on the contemplative life. Through her spiritual practices and teachings, she tapped into profound spiritual reservoirs and encouraged people to cultivate a deeper connection with the divine. Her ability to stir the waters and foster connections is evident in her efforts to establish and reform religious communities, by emphasizing the importance of prayer, contemplation, and inner transformation.

Chapter Nine

Eris enables our diversity consciousness, as we learn to value everything and everyone for who they truly are. She encourages us to simultaneously see ourselves in an uncompromising way and be inclusive in our world view. We tend to fool ourselves and overlook our shortcomings just to get through each day, but Eris draws her strength from the unflinching nature of her understanding. It's all valuable to her and we'll only be complete and embrace our full power when we accept our multifaceted nature.

Similarly, in the outer world, Eris wants everyone to be valued and included. And she has no time for judgment or comparison. She teaches us to maintain a steady spirit through all crises by being open to the promptings of love and sympathy. This is vital for our spiritual growth because it gives us the strength and courage necessary to take the spiritual risks required. It encourages us to develop an open heart, which is essential for personal transformation and expanded consciousness. Our lives go through different phases, but through compassion we are able to support ourselves and one another through any challenge: and by facing the challenge we learn to transmute that effort into love.

In mythology Eris was the warrior sister of Mars and was considered the goddess of discord. The siblings were always allied in battle together and Eris was invariably the last one to leave. So, she can encourage us to rise to any challenge and to stand our ground until we are the last warrior on the battlefield. But while this tenaciousness can be a great benefit, we don't always need to slay everyone else to make our point. We have to understand when we have already won, and when to leave well enough alone.

Where Mars is fighting mundane battles, Eris' challenge is on a more esoteric level. In modern astrology Pluto is considered to be the higher octave of Mars, so we can look at Eris as the higher octave of Pluto. She steps up his transformative energy to a fierce grace through which everything in our lives is opened to the light and can be transmuted into love.

If we are still at the personal planet level of consciousness, however, and sensing this influence unconsciously, we are likely to get caught up in the battles in our lives. Or we might actively seek them out by getting on our high horse about what is important for us, or speaking out about something, whether this is appropriate or not. These confrontations shine light on parts of ourselves that we have denied or pushed into the unconscious, or simply taken for granted. We need discord to grow. It's only in the to-and-fro of opposing points of view that change occurs. Eris doesn't really cause trouble; she just shines a light on the need for change by provoking our natural reactions, so we can see where they lead.

At this level, she is teaching us to stop being fooled, or

to stop fooling ourselves. At the same time, she is also likely encouraging us to be competitive, and to take any advantage when we can, because 'everyone else does!'. When we buy into the rampant greed and selfishness of the capitalist system, it convinces us that there is no other way - that the rat race is the only game in town, so we join it with Eris's whole-heartedness. Or we might go to any lengths to be included in some enterprise or social group, compromising ourselves in the process. Or we could be unable to compromise and so not allowed to participate. As a result, we may feel alienated and excluded from meaningful social interaction.

As we adopt a more spiritual approach, we learn that our strife can be delt with by accepting the opposing point of view, and that without strife, we can live in harmony. This diversity consciousness enables us to understand that the problem is seeing the opposing view as a challenge. To accept an opposing view, we have to grow spiritually, so that our belief is not challenged by a lack of the same belief in another. At this level, Eris becomes the goddess of pluralism, enabling us each to believe what works for us.

As we develop our spiritual approach, we can embrace a practice of love and sympathy. We realize that growing spiritually and pushing the boundaries of our understanding is challenging and uncertain, requiring a willingness to step out of our comfort zone and face potential obstacles and we know that love and sympathy gives us the motivation and support we need to navigate these risks. We learn to see clearly without preconceptions, and this helps us keep our body and mind in harmony so that we are healthy and happy.

The mischief or misbehaviour that we indulged in at the unconscious level, is clearly off limits now that we see our lives in a higher light.

And, at the spiritually evolved level, we understand Eris' fierce grace for the transmuted love that it is. We understand that it is through engaging and doing the work, that this effort is transmuted into love. And this gives us a female power that we can bring to bear in our lives. Where the male power of Pluto and Mars is coercive, Eris' power is more sensitive and gentle in its engagement, but it rises to meet the needs of any challenge.

When we embrace her fierce grace, she brings a sacred wisdom into our lives. This may manifest as a spirit guide who can help us with sacred knowledge. Or as a connection to our inner guide, the part of us that knows where we are in our dance between karma and dharma, and what is best in each situation. At this level, we become a truth-telling trickster, able to get our message through by crafting it perfectly for each person. We value everyone as they are, accepting everything and neither comparing nor judging.

Too Hot to Handle

Eris brings sacred truth into our lives, and we have to be ready to 'handle it', or we will blow a fuse. Just like the yogis of old who practiced devoutly to be able to channel divine grace, work is required to enable and integrate these new outer planet energies. We do the work by learning to ground Eris's light in practical ways in our daily lives.

When we're not ready to do this, we are likely to project it out and tell everyone else what they should do. It is all too easy to see what others should do with their lives, but much harder to turn that transpersonal gaze on ourselves.

So, Eris brings us sacred truth, but we have to be able to hear her message, and we have to ground it in reality by doing something about it. This is the secret to handling her heat, we have to embody her insight by acting on it, and then she becomes an endless source of sensitive strength.

Eris Consciousness Challenges

This section might be better titled, 'Dealing with Eris Consciousness Challenges' because she frequently manifests in our lives as challenges to our consciousness that we have to deal with. These exercises will be best focused in the area of your life represented by your Eris house position.

1. **Stop fooling yourself.** We often fool ourselves by what we say to others. To the question *"How are you?"* we say, *"I'm fine,"* rather than articulating what's really going on. Start self-correcting these self-fooling moments by being brave enough to be more authentic.

2. **Accept the opposing view.** If you're in a confrontation, examine what would need to change on either side to reach an accommodation. Is there a way to allow the opposing view so you can both live in harmony? If there is, make moves to enable that. If there isn't, quit the dispute.

3. **Practice compassion in action.** Reach out to someone in your world who is in need and lend a helping hand to enable their survival. This is a practical way to transmute life into love.

4. **Ground Eris practically.** Next time you can see something clearly in an Eris way, look for what small and immediate step you can take to manifest that vision. And then take that step and don't second guess it. That step leads to another, so take that and keep taking appropriate action to manifest your clarity. It is through acting that we ground her sacred wisdom.

5. **Reveal a hidden facet.** Search out a neglected side of yourself that you would like to develop and give yourself permission to find a way to do that. Then take the first step to do it. Tell yourself that, *"It's good if this is incongruous with my normal life, because it is enabling greater authenticity."*

6. **Know when to get off your high horse.** When you next find yourself rising to an Eris challenge, stay sensitive to when you have already won. There is a point at which continuing the battle turns it into a strategic defeat, by arousing more enmity than it allays. And when that moment comes, although there may still be stragglers on the battlefield, declare victory and de-escalate. This is hard to do, because the power is with you and there is still work to do, but you can transmute that into love and sympathy by pulling your head in and leaving well enough alone.

Eris in the Houses

First House

With Eris in the 1st House, diversity consciousness is central to our world view. This is the house of self and our mission is to trust ourselves. With this placement, we will be constantly evolving out of the current limits on our consciousness and opening ourselves to see beyond the finite bounds of our perception. This is the house of how others perceive us and, with this placement, we will do things differently from other people and will likely be seen either as a troublemaker, or as a truth-teller.

At the unconscious level, however, we are likely to argue back when challenged, whether this is appropriate or not, which is likely to antagonize people. And, at this level, our self-interest may make us greedy, and we could fall into workaholism, or we might try to win approval to get ahead.

When we are on the spiritual path, we can develop our self-awareness and free ourselves from addictions to success or status. At this level, we understand that we can't take it with us and we learn to apply our full resourcefulness in life.

Like British author, J.K. Rowling, known for promoting diversity and inclusivity in the Harry Potter series. Having faced multiple rejections from publishers before finding success with her debut novel, *Harry Potter and the Philosopher's Stone,* her resourcefulness is evident in her personal journey as a writer. Despite early financial struggles, she persevered and used her imagination and creativity to build a rich and intricate fictional world that captivated readers worldwide.

And, at the spiritually evolved level, we can see clearly without preconceptions, and we keep our body and mind in harmony so that health and happiness prevails. At this level we will have a personal sense of emergence. Through love and sympathy, we will be able to maintain the life of our spirit in times of crisis.

Like influential Indian spiritual leader and teacher, Yogi Bhajan, who introduced Kundalini Yoga to the Western world. He was the founder of the Healthy, Happy, Holy Organization, which promoted healthy living by emphasizing a balanced diet, regular exercise, and practices to enhance mental and emotional well-being. Kundalini Yoga is known for its dynamic and transformative nature, helping practitioners achieve physical strength, mental clarity, emotional balance, and spiritual upliftment.

Second House

With Eris in the 2nd House, we will have clear priorities regarding matters of love and money, as we understand that we can't take it with us and we apply our full resourcefulness in life. With this placement, we will have an alternative attitude towards wealth and material possessions, and may wish to live off the grid, understanding that 'sharing and caring' is key to our ability to provide for ourselves.

At the unconscious level, however, our greed and lack of spiritual regard for life could lead us to indulge in sensual pleasures and use our resources to try and dominate our social sphere. At this level, we are likely to be status oriented and may suffer from a lack of boundaries and a general sense of being forsaken, condemned, or abandoned. We might find ourselves speaking our mind at times when it is not appropriate and suffer consequences as a result.

Like American comedian, Roseanne Barr, known for her unique and often controversial comedic style. She has been lauded for her ability to push boundaries and tackle taboo subjects in her comedy. However, she has faced significant controversy due to her public statements, particularly through her use of social media, which have sometimes been criticized for being offensive, racist, or promoting conspiracy theories. These controversial statements have led to significant backlash and have had a negative impact on her career.

When we move onto the spiritual path, we can learn to keep our body and mind in harmony so that health and happiness prevails. As we do, we develop an inclusive world view, understanding that our sense of self-worth is dependent on the degree to which we are faithful to our values.

Like American author Ray Bradbury, whose science fiction spoke to broader societal issues, including censorship, social conformity, and the dangers of technology. His stories explored the consequences of neglecting the human spirit and the importance of maintaining a balance between technological advancements and emotional well-being. They frequently highlighted the value of individuality and the potential consequences of suppressing diverse perspectives.

At the spiritually evolved level, we can see clearly without preconceptions and can overcome crises through compassion. At this level, our diversity consciousness can provide safety, security, nourishment, or emotional support to those who may not know how to solve their problems themselves.

Like internationally renowned American intuitive, author, and public speaker, Linda Georgian, who approached her work as a professional intuitive as a way to educate and help people. Her book, *Your Guardian Angels,* was popular worldwide and published in several languages. She gave talks internationally in which she focused on health, spirituality, and personal empowerment. She also gave private intuitive readings to thousands of clients and consulted with law enforcement on missing persons cases.

Third House

With Eris in the 3rd House, the chaos in our minds brings ideas together when we give ourselves the freedom to think outside the box. With this placement, we will have a strong voice and can maintain our spirit steadily through all crises by being open to love and sympathy.

At the unconscious level, however, we are likely to have a more superficial approach, overlooking details and arguing back when challenged, whether this is appropriate or not.

At this level, we may lack a spiritual regard for life, and we may get caught in reactive thinking patterns. We need to learn to stop being fooled, or to stop fooling ourselves.

When we are on the spiritual path, we recognise the potency of our ideas and can adopt a sharing and caring approach to making connections. At this level, we may have a personal sense of emergence, understanding what is off balance in society and feel that it is our place to speak about this.

Like British novelist and Nobel laureate, Doris Lessing, who explored themes of inequality, racism, and the struggle for individual freedom and expression, all of which highlighted societal imbalances. Her books depict the struggles faced by people who challenge established norms and seek their own personal freedom, often questioning and critiquing oppressive systems and societal constraints in the process. She encourages her readers to examine the complexities of human existence and contemplate the possibilities for individual growth, liberation, and self-expression.

Then, at the spiritually evolved level, we value each person for who they are, accepting everything and neither comparing nor judging. At this level, our diversity consciousness enables us to be a thought leader, writing or speaking about our ideas.

Like prominent Tibetan Buddhist teacher and spiritual leader, Shamar Rinpoche, who emphasized the importance of meditation and mindfulness as powerful tools for achieving inner peace, clarity, and spiritual transformation. He guided his students to recognize and actualize their innate potential for awakening and spiritual growth, and provided teachings and practices related to the nature of mind, and which emphasize the inherent qualities of awareness and wisdom that lie within every individual.

Fourth House

With Eris in the 4th House, we are liberated from addictions to success or status, and have the courage to break away from traditions and find ourselves. We may feel like we are the odd one out in the family and have childhood experiences of unequal power distribution causing problems in the home.

At the unconscious level, we may have a sense of being abandoned by family members and need to be careful of trying to win approval, or of developing co-dependent relationships. We might also have a lack of boundaries, and as a result may feel used by others.

When we are on the spiritual path, however, we begin to see the karmic baggage we brought into this life and recognize how past conditions have contributed to our current problems. At this level, we can work through this karma, enabling us to keep our body and mind in harmony so that health and happiness prevails.

Russian chess grandmaster, world chess champion, and political activist, Garry Kasparov, exemplifies this karmic vision. He has frequently criticized the lingering effects of the Soviet legacy, emphasizing how the suppression of dissent, and the lack of democratic institutions have contributed to Russia's ongoing challenges. His diversity consciousness encouraged him to promote democratic reforms, hold leaders accountable for past actions, and foster a culture that prioritizes and protects individual freedoms.

And, at the spiritually evolved level, we understand our karmic lesson for this lifetime, and have an ability to help those in need by providing safety, security, nourishment, or emotional support. At this level, we understand that non-judgmental attitudes help others to trust us.

Like well-known American psychic medium, Lisa Williams, who has dedicated her career to helping people connect with their loved ones who have passed away. She offers readings, workshops, and courses aimed at exploring spiritual growth and healing. Her approach is often described as compassionate and non-judgmental, creating a safe space for individuals seeking closure and guidance.

Fifth House

With Eris in the 5th House, we will be a different drummer in our creative self-expression, inspiring others and provoking change by upsetting limited and antiquated structures of consciousness. With this placement, we feel the potency and inclusive nature of our life-force in our love and the way we raise our children.

At the unconscious level, however, we may not feel this potency and may instead feel forsaken or abandoned. As a result, we might throw ourselves into love affairs and the pursuit of pleasure, or into risk-taking and gambling, because of a lack of spiritual regard for life.

When we are on the spiritual path, we can maintain the life of the spirit steadily through all crises by staying open to love and sympathy. This encourages the development of an open heart, which is essential for personal transformation. At this level, we can see clearly without preconceptions, and we have the courage to take the spiritual risks necessary to grow in consciousness.

Like American occultist, author, and spiritual teacher, Dolores Ashcroft-Nowicki, who has studied Hermeticism, Kabbalah, Tarot, Alchemy, and other disciplines, and developed her own unique approach. She encourages direct experience of the divine, and the integration of esoteric principles into daily life. By fearlessly delving into esoteric practices and traditions, she has contributed to the expansion of esoteric knowledge and spiritual growth, and her openness to love and sympathy has enabled the sharing of these insights.

At the spiritually evolved level, we can transmute life into love, and value each person for who they truly are. At this level, we can keep our body and mind in harmony so that health and happiness prevail, and we might become a revered teacher.

Like renowned Indian spiritual teacher, Nityananda, who believed in the inherent divinity within all individuals and taught about self-realization and the unity of all beings. Understanding that true liberation comes from recognizing our essential nature beyond the limitations of the mind and body, he emphasized the importance of accepting oneself and others without judgment or discrimination.

Sixth House

With Eris in the 6th House, we have a potent way of responding to everyday crises, overcoming them through compassion. With this placement, we are likely to feel oppressed by the daily grind of normal jobs and may choose self-employment instead, where our maverick style is an advantage. This is also the house of wellness and health, and we are our own best health advisor when we listen to our inner guide and find a harmony in our daily rhythm.

At the unconscious level, however, we may not want to do the work of looking after ourselves, ignoring issues like personal hygiene until we become physically sick. Or we might find ourselves in a health crisis which is not managed well by our healthcare provider.

When we are on the spiritual path, we can adopt a more caretaking approach to our daily rhythm and feel a rise in vitality as a result. At this level, we might choose to have more agency by doing volunteer work, rather than paid work, understanding that helping others has its own rewards.

Like German spiritual teacher and author, Bo Yin Ra, who taught that by engaging in selfless acts, we can elevate our consciousness and experience a deeper connection with the Divine. In his books, he highlighted the importance of transcending self-centeredness and cultivating a genuine concern for the well-being of others. He believed that acts of selfless service contribute to the evolution of consciousness, fostering a sense of unity, love, and higher understanding.

At the spiritually evolved level, our diversity consciousness enables us to compassionately serve our community, providing safety, security, nourishment, and emotional support to those who may not know how to solve their problems themselves.

Like Dutch faith healer and counselor, Greet Hofmans, who believed in the power of energy, and of the interconnectedness of mind, body, and spirit. She became known for her work providing emotional support and guidance to people, including members of the Dutch royal family. Her work emphasized the importance of addressing emotional well-being and understanding the mind, body, and spirit in a holistic way, to achieve health and harmony.

Seventh House

With Eris in the 7th House, we have clear priorities regarding matters of love and money in our one-to-one relationships, and an ability to overcome crises through compassion. With this placement we can see through the details in our contracts and official documents.

At the unconscious level, however, we are likely to quarrel with our partners about issues of status or openness, and to argue back, whether this is appropriate or not. We may also have a lack of boundaries and a feeling of being used. There may be an uneven power dynamic in our relationships, or we may have a superficial and status-oriented approach which, either way, can lead to separation and lawsuits. At this level, we are learning to stop being fooled, or to stop fooling ourselves and we need to be careful of trying to win approval, or of forming co-dependent relationships.

When we are on the spiritual path, we can see ourselves and our partners more clearly and this diversity consciousness enables a more cooperative and sharing approach. At this level, our non-judgmental attitude is the key to our partners trusting us.

Like spiritual teacher and leader in the Siddha Yoga tradition, Gurumayi, whose teachings emphasize selfless service and foster a sense of unity and cooperation. She talks about the importance of nurturing positive, loving relationships with others. She encourages her followers to communicate openly, listen attentively, and work together to resolve conflicts in a compassionate and respectful manner. By promoting selfless service, unity, and cooperation, her teachings aim to create a sense of collective responsibility and shared well-being.

And, at the spiritually evolved level, we can transmute life into love, by valuing our partners in their naked splendor as we accept everything and neither compare nor judge them. At this level, our diversity consciousness fosters a community of like-minded people through our relationships.

Like prominent astrologer and writer, Alan Leo, who believed that astrology had a spiritual and philosophical dimension beyond mere fortune-telling. He emphasized using it as a tool for self-understanding, personal growth, and spiritual development. His approach aimed to empower individuals by helping them align with their true selves and life purpose. He founded the Astrological Lodge in London, providing a platform for education and fostering a community of like-minded individuals.

Eighth House

With Eris in the 8th House, we understand the law of karma, and we get that we can't take it with us, so we need to apply our full resourcefulness in this life. This placement opens us to see beyond the finite bounds of our current perception and puts us in touch with deep truths.

At the unconscious level, however, we are more likely to have a sense of being forsaken, condemned, or abandoned. We may compensate for these feelings by acting in a greedy way, becoming a workaholic, or by getting addicted to success or status. At this level, inheritances, insurance payments and loans can be contentious areas. We might also have an interest in kinky sex. Or we could have a desire to sow chaos, as a way of empowering ourselves, but karma will always catch up with us and so this approach could bring losses and debt.

When we are on the spiritual path, however, we will have a personal sense of emergence. At this level, we have open and clear priorities regarding matters of sex and joint resources, and we are in touch with deep truths and can bring them into our world, enriching and catalyzing our collective energies in the process.

Like American author, astrologer, and spiritual teacher, Barbara Hand Clow, who has written extensively on astrology, mythology, and spiritual transformation. Her books delve into deep truths and provide spiritual insights, aiming to expand awareness and inspire a new understanding of the world. Through her books and teachings, she has sought to bridge the gap between spirituality and everyday life, encouraging us to explore our own spiritual paths and expand our consciousness.

At the spiritually evolved level, our deep truths will enliven the collective and inspire new faith. At this level, our diversity consciousness can sustain our spirit through all crises by maintaining an openness to love and sympathy.

Like the Indian philosopher, poet, and yogi, Sri Aurobindo, whose teachings emphasize the importance of love, compassion, and understanding in spiritual growth and the transformation of consciousness. He believed that love and sympathy are integral to human development and have the power to heal and uplift both individuals and society as a whole.

Ninth House

With Eris in the 9th House, we will search for the meaning of things and have big thoughts and big ideas which will be different from the norm and are likely to be considered radical. With this placement, we open to the light, and we finally get that we can't take it with us and instead apply our full resourcefulness in living fully.

At the unconscious level, however, we may instead feel oppressed by religion, rejecting spirituality and calling ourselves an atheist. This could lead us to speak our mind, whether this is appropriate or not. A superficial and antagonistic approach is also likely to get us into confrontations in higher education settings, or when we are traveling. At this level, we may have a general lack of spiritual regard for life and a sense of being forsaken, condemned, or abandoned.

This is exemplified by the work of American author, Stephen King, known for his contribution to the horror and suspense genres. He delves deep into the psyche of his characters, into their motivations and fears, making them feel authentic and multidimensional. His stories frequently explore themes such as fear, loss, trauma, and the darker aspects of human nature, and they combine ordinary, everyday settings with supernatural elements, creating a sense that horror can exist just beneath the surface of our normal lives.

Yet when we are on the spiritual path, we revel in the contentious debate of philosophical ideas, as these provide rich opportunities for our growth. Through this we can become a truth-teller, gaining a personal sense of emergence, and taking volatile ideas and baking them into new form through our work over time.

Like Russian-American writer and philosopher, Ayn Rand, known for her individualistic and objectivist philosophy. She challenged conventional moral and ethical norms, advocating that we should each pursue our own values and reject altruism as morally superior. Her writings defended the rights of individuals to think for themselves, make choices based on reason, and pursue their own life goals without interference from the collective or government.

And, at the spiritually evolved level, we can see clearly without preconceptions, thus enabling us to develop a deep wisdom. As we shine this light into the world, people will be attracted by this wisdom and we may become a revered teacher.

Like Indian philosopher and spiritual teacher, U.G. Krishnamurti, known for his radical and unconventional approach to enlightenment. His philosophy emphasizes the importance of direct and immediate experiential understanding, rather than relying on beliefs or concepts. He held that the mind was the source of all suffering, and that true freedom lies in the dissolution of the self-structure created by psychological thought patterns. He advocated for a natural and spontaneous way of living, free from the constructs and constraints of society and ideology, emphasizing the importance of self-inquiry and relying on our own direct experiences and observations. He taught that we need to be present in the here and now, rather than seeking enlightenment or spiritual progress in the future.

Tenth House

With Eris in the 10th House, we seek a social role that challenges the limiting and antiquated social structures and the prevailing collective consciousness that we find around us. With this placement, we have an ability to help those who have been left out, providing safety, security, nourishment, or emotional support, especially to those who may not know how to solve their problems themselves.

At the unconscious level, however, we might have a more status-oriented approach and become a workaholic, or we could react against authority figures, speaking out and achieving notoriety for our discordant views.

When we are on the spiritual path, we can see clearly without preconceptions, and we keep our body and mind in harmony so that health and happiness prevails. At this level, we realize that helping others has its own rewards and non-judgmental attitudes are the key to building trusted social foundations, so that we can all live in harmony.

Like American actress and comedian, Lily Tomlin, whose comedy often highlights the absurdities of societal norms and prejudices, urging audiences to question and challenge their own biases. Known for her versatility and comedic genius, she has masterfully portrayed characters from various backgrounds, often challenging stereotypes and shedding light on the complexities of human experiences. Her humour encourages self-reflection and introspection, reminding people not to take themselves too seriously and fostering an atmosphere of light-heartedness and acceptance.

At the spiritually evolved level, we can be liberated from addictions to success or status and can overcome social crises through compassion. We learn to transmute life into love, likely gaining recognition, community power, and prestige through this work. At this level, our diversity consciousness enables us to see the interconnectedness of everyone.

Like prominent American spiritual teacher and author, Ram Dass, known for his work on consciousness, mindfulness, and compassion. He encouraged his followers to cultivate a loving and compassionate attitude towards themselves and others, recognizing the inherent unity and interconnectedness of all beings. His book, *Be Here Now* introduced Eastern spiritual teachings to a Western audience in a relatable and accessible way. It combined memoir, philosophy, and practical guidance, as well as offering insights into the nature of the self, mindfulness practices, and the importance of living in the present moment.

Eleventh House

With Eris in the 11th House, we will seek out a group of like-minded friends who share our inclusive view of community. With this placement, we have big dreams and an ability to be non-judgemental and help those in need through support groups, or to reach out to those who may be excluded from these groups.

At the unconscious level, however, our need to belong might lead us to get involved with radical groups, or those with a chip on their shoulder. Or we might be excluded from groups altogether, which is likely to give us a feeling of being forsaken, condemned, or abandoned. At this level, we are learning to stop being fooled by our connections or to stop fooling ourselves.

When we move onto the spiritual path, however, we begin a process of self-realization and learn to see clearly without preconceptions. As our diversity consciousness develops, we can adopt a sharing and caring approach to our friendships. At this level, we seek out groups that help us keep our body and our mind in harmony, so we are healthy and happy.

Like American astronomer, astrophysicist, and cosmologist, Carl Sagan, who wrote about the interconnectedness of all life in his book, *Cosmos: A Personal Voyage.* The book, and the accompanying television series, explored a wide range of scientific topics, including astronomy, cosmology, and biology, in an accessible and engaging manner. His series reached a massive audience and played a pivotal role in sparking interest in science worldwide.

Then, at the spiritually evolved level, we will be open to the promptings of love and sympathy and have a potent connection with our community. At this level, we can feel the currents in the collective consciousness, and our open heart enables us to maintain our contact with Spirit steadily through any crisis of consciousness that may arise.

Like well-known astrologer, author, and lecturer, Georgia Stathis, who specializes in financial astrology, analyzing the correlation between astrological patterns and economic trends. By connecting the patterns in the sky with everyday life, she aims to help people navigate challenges and make informed decisions in both personal and business areas. Her work in this area is highly regarded and she has provided valuable insights to individuals, investors, and businesses seeking guidance in financial matters.

Twelfth House

With Eris in the 12th House, our diversity consciousness enables us to see how our subconscious habit patterns exclude us from participating fully in our community. This enables us to work through these issues so we can apply our full resourcefulness in life.

At the unconscious level, however, we may sabotage our relationships by not working through this baggage, or we could suppress our discordant energy in an effort to conform.

At this level, we likely have a lack of spiritual regard for life, and may deceive ourselves or others, or undermine our efforts, by speaking out inappropriately. We need to be careful of trying to win approval, or of not being rigorous about our boundaries, because, either way, we could end up feeling used.

When we are on the spiritual path, we begin to understand that this baggage is karmic, and we learn to overcome it through compassion and adopting a less ego-centered approach. At this level, we are sensitive to the bigger spiritual reality, and we might have an ability to help people find comfort, healing, and understanding through that contact.

Like renowned American medium, Arthur Ford, known for his compassionate approach in connecting with the spirit world. He would enter trance states, allowing a spirit known as "Fletcher" to speak through him and deliver messages to people seeking contact with their deceased loved ones. He gave many public demonstrations, gaining widespread attention and attracting large audiences. He was known for his ability to provide detailed and accurate information about the spirits he communicated with, often conveying highly specific details that were confirmed by the recipients of the messages.

And, at the spiritually evolved level, we have a deep connection with the spirit world and may experience revelatory events or miracles. At this level, we may have a powerful prophetic spiritual voice and an ability to channel the higher wisdom.

Like esteemed astrologer and author, Ariel Guttman, known for her work in Evolutionary Astrology, a branch that focuses on the soul's growth over multiple lifetimes. This approach aims to provide insights into the individual's soul evolution and the karmic lessons they may be encountering in their current life. One of her most notable works is *Astrology and the Evolution of Consciousness: Volume One,* which delves into the spiritual and psychological dimensions of astrology, providing readers with tools to explore their own soul's journey and understand their life choices and challenges from a larger perspective.

SEDNA

Chapter Ten

And, finally, way out beyond all the other planets, in a huge elliptical orbit, we find the new outer limit of our solar system, Sedna. Here the ego consciousness morphs into an ineffable universal consciousness, which is heart-centered, and protective in a transpersonal, big picture way.

With Sedna we learn to let go of the physical realm and allow transcendence to a new holistic spiritual consciousness where we learn to allow love and harmony, and nurture abundance. Sedna is always trying to get us on the spiritual path, and she will use any mechanism at her disposal to achieve this. All options are available to her.

So, when we are at the personal planet consciousness, she brings transcendent crises into our lives which force us to let go of our old consciousness framework and transcend to a new spiritual consciousness. There is no solution to a Sedna crisis. But, by being counterintuitive and letting go early, we can avoid repeated pain. Pain is a signal that we need to change something. And, when we listen to it early and make those changes, we will have less of it in our lives.

If we are having a Sedna crisis, we will be experiencing repeated pain in the area of our lives represented by her house position in our birth chart, or by the house she is currently transiting through, or the houses opposite her natal or transit position. The important thing, when we realize it is a Sedna crisis, is to be counter-intuitive and let go of the problem, rather than try to solve it.

Letting go is very hard to do, because we are brought up to be responsible, and the responsible thing is to face up to our issues, rather than turn our back on them. But Sedna issues can't be solved within our current consciousness framework because they are designed to be transcended, to lift us out of our lower consciousness, or to shock or force us out if necessary. Transcendence is scary, because we don't know where it will take us, but Saturnian solutions won't solve Sedna crises. Only letting go of them will free us.

A persistent health crisis is one way Sedna can set us up for transcendence. These are crises caused by our lifestyle being out of balance with what our soul needs. Sedna health crises are the ones which change our lives. We are not the same afterwards as we were before. When we are experiencing a Sedna health crisis, the answer to our physical problem is to concentrate on our spiritual growth.

Spiritual growth is always good anyway, right? Yes, but this will likely also mean practically changing our lives in some way. The spiritual and practical changes go together like opposite sides of a coin, but we have to let the spiritual changes lead the process. It's up to us how we respond, and if we've solved the crisis, it is because we found a more spiritual perspective.

Sedna's wakeup call can also manifest through situations where we are victimized or alienated in some way. The pressure of these experiences pushes us to grow in ways that our soul intends. Victimization is a role relationship, and we are consciously or unconsciously complicit in these relationships. So, if we don't like it, we have to make the choice to let go of that role and find out who we are without it in our life. That might seem obvious, but we wouldn't be in that situation if it was. We need the victim relationship as an evolutionary impulse for our growth, and it's only when we have embodied that soul intention, that we can let it go.

We might experience Sedna's transcendent grace through other forms of trauma and suffering which seem to be unrelenting. Or we could feel an unbearable pressure in some area of our lives. Or that we are caught in quicksand in some way, unable to get out of our situation and sinking further in with every movement. Again, we can't get out of the crisis by struggling, that just compounds the problem. We have to let go of the crisis in order transcend it. These are all ways that Sedna can push us to adopt a more spiritual approach.

As we develop spiritually, Sedna teaches us to keep our heart open in what we are increasingly realizing is a sort of hell that we are currently living through. Hell is a place of darkness, hopelessness, and despair, where souls are separated from light, goodness, and any form of divine presence, and many of us experience the world like that today. We are still very early in our consciousness development as a species, and we have to keep our heart open for our benefit, and for everyone else's benefit, in this difficult phase.

To do this, we need to nurture our sense of humor. A sense of humor is a wonderful tool on the spiritual path, because it allows us to release baggage and lighten our load on our soul's path of destiny. At this level, Sedna encourages us to beat our drum and sing our song to life. We need to do the soul-based work that we are here to do, and this will lead us through a fated transcendence to a more transpersonal consciousness.

And, at the spiritually evolved level we can embrace our spiritual destiny and joyfully do what our soul wants to do. At this level, she brings us transcendent peace, and the ability to nurture abundance. When we are in tune with our soul needs, our material needs are manifest in our lives at each moment. It may not be what we want, but it is what we need. By having the courage to embrace our soul needs and nurture them, we invite abundance into our lives.

We also learn to allow love and harmony at this level. Love and harmony can only occur when we allow them. We do this by dealing with anything that isn't love - the lower Sedna issues - and simultaneously making the space for love to exist. We have to believe in it, in the face of the many others who seemingly don't. We have to allow it.

At this highest level, we can let go of the ego's need to be special, and just enjoy our place in the sun. And that enables us to let go of all the baggage cluttering up our consciousness and let in fresh ideas and energy.

Embracing our Soul's Path of Destiny

We can think of Sedna as the higher octave of Ceres, our newly reclassified inner dwarf planet, who orbits between

Mars and Jupiter. Ceres is our ability to love and be loved. At both a basic level and in the bigger sense of the word, she represents what we need to feed and nourish ourselves.

And we can think of Ceres as the higher octave of the Moon, our emotional center. The Moon is the other luminary in our chart, where we see ourselves reflected in each moment. The Moon mediates our survival through each of those moments, and Ceres talks of the process of those moments and mediates our survival over time.

Sedna steps this heart-centered energy all the way out to the new limit of our solar system, so she talks of our survival over lifetimes. I call her *our Soul's Path of Destiny* because, if we accept that our soul incarnates over a number of lifetimes and that it has a purpose to grow through those incarnations, then in this life, our soul purpose is shown by the Sedna placement.

The only choice with Sedna, is to embrace each step on our soul's path of destiny and do the dharmic work required. We need to accept in our heart that everything that happens is perfectly crafted for our soul growth.

Sedna Consciousness Challenges

There are no easy exercises with Sedna because we're dealing with our soul needs. And she already sends us lessons which are perfectly crafted for our growth, so these exercises are focused on ways to work effectively with the lessons she sends us, so we can better on-board this energy into our lives.

1. **Nurture your sense of humor.** Seek out situations that make you laugh. And when you do, notice the release of karmic baggage that the laughter enables. A weight is lifted from you, and you can go lighter on your soul's path of destiny.

2. **Let go of repeated pain.** Easy to say, and hard to do, but if you are experiencing repeated pain in some area of your life, let go of whatever is causing that pain. However central it is to your life, find a way to let it go and transcend to a new understanding of who you are without that pain. Scary though it may be, you can trust that it will be a healthier and more spiritual expression of you.

3. **Deal with victimization.** This is a role relationship, so identify the victimizer, and then identify why you buy into that relationship, and see if you can source that need elsewhere. As in the last exercise you have to embody the soul intention and let go of the victimizer to find who you are without that in your life.

4. **Turn trauma into a blessing.** If Sedna is manifesting as endless trauma, or if you are trying to understand current or past trauma in your life, it is important to embrace this trauma as valuable work in your spiritual development. As you embody the understanding that it is perfectly tailored for your soul growth, you will be able to look back and see the trauma as a blessing in disguise.

5. **Solving Sedna illnesses.** If you are experiencing an ongoing health crisis, consider if it is being caused by your lifestyle being out of balance with your

spiritual needs. If it is, bring spiritual solutions to bear on the physical problem, or concentrate on your spiritual growth as the answer.

6. **Allow love and harmony.** If you are having difficulty with this, identify what issue from your soul's heritage is cramping your style. There is karma to resolve. Work on that and resolve it! Then believe in love once more, even in the face of all the non-believers.

7. **Nurture abundance.** Notice what manifests in your life in each moment. It may not be what you want, but it is what you need. Find the courage to embrace that and nurture it, because that is the source of your abundance.

Sedna in the Houses

First House

With Sedna in the 1st House, we are on a spiritual quest to investigate what it is to be uniquely ourselves, as well as the relationship between us and the cultural and physical environment in which we find ourselves. With this placement, we are truly on a quest of self-development.

Various influences in our lives will motivate us to begin this quest, but they are all likely to involve some form of pressure, which could give us a sense of alienation, or victimization. Or we might deny our own needs in the face of the demands from those around us, until this position no longer becomes tenable, and we must break out.

Science fiction writer Philip K. Dick exemplifies this, with his stories typically focusing on the fragile nature of what is real and the construction of personal identity within that tenuous reality. They often become surreal fantasies, as the main characters slowly discover that their everyday world is actually an illusion assembled by powerful external entities, by vast political conspiracies, or by the changes in circumstances of an unreliable narrator.

Karl Marx, who also had this placement, posited that self-development begins for everyone with an experience of internal alienation, and he built his entire social theory on this premise. He believed that the alienation of labor occurs when the makers of things are separated from their ownership of them. Growth motivated by internal alienation-of-self is definitely a signature of Sedna in the first.

A buildup of pressure is normally required to motivate us on our self-discovery quest, because we tend to be afraid to plumb the depths of our personality. We want to see ourselves in a good light, so we overlook inherent problems. However, our Sedna spiritual quest always demands we acknowledge just how bad things really are and start from there.

Because Sedna is the new outer limit of our solar system, she replaces Saturn's limiting principle in the birth chart, with one that is much further out. For those with a strong Sedna signature, the Saturnian rules have no meaning, so at the unconscious level we might conceive of a hair-brained scheme that is totally grounded from our point of view, but off the planet from everyone else's perspective and out of cinque with the physical world around us.

While we are unconscious of the energy, we might assert ourselves at times as if our sense of self depended on it. This provocation will invoke correspondingly strong reactions from others in our environment, which can generate a victim and victimizer relationship in which we might play either role.

We likely have a deep well of personality traits to mine for our growth and know no boundaries in uncovering the taboo underbelly of our own and others' lives. We may even use this as the raw material for our profession, like Marx, or Dick. Or like stand-up comedian, Joan Rivers, who delivered a rapid-fire mix of gossip and insults in her shows, flaunting taboos, and ridiculing flaws and neuroses, as she built a rich comedy empire.

Because we are exploring ourselves as the canvas of our growth, there will likely be times that we need to withdraw deep within ourselves in order to sort through our thoughts and feelings. Through this process it is important to maintain reference points to the wider society, so we don't get lost in ourselves.

When we succeed in attaining a more spiritual outlook on life, our sense of self is not threatened so easily, and we become more secure in ourselves. Like evangelist, Billy Graham, who was born again as a teenager and, despite the fact that he has preached to more people in live audiences than anyone else in history, still ministered from a quietly confident personal level.

If we haven't worked through all the baser sides of Sedna, however, these can still manifest as spiritual traps on the path to enlightenment. One Swami with this placement was one of a select group of disciples chosen by his guru as the collective leaders of the movement. However, on the guru's death, he started preaching that he was the chosen one and, when he was thrown out by the governing council, he formed a breakaway movement that flourished until he was caught molesting a young male follower.

As we plumb the depths of our individuality and grow in consciousness, we will begin to understand ourselves and the web of interactions that we live amongst on a more transpersonal level. At this level, we can live our lives in ways that exemplify both our deepest spiritual needs as an individual and also serve the wider society.

Second House

With Sedna in the 2nd House, we are on a spiritual quest to investigate the material reality in which we find ourselves. At the ego level, material reality is often equated with possessions and money, but it is better thought of as the resources, including the inner resources, that are available to us.

Some pressure in our life will motivate this resource mission. We might be born into a family with scarce resources, or we might suffer a financial hardship where we lose money we already have. We could also be materially dependent on someone, or someone could be dependent on us.

At the unconscious level, we might have a sense of injustice, or of being disadvantaged by our situation. But as we embrace the Sedna energy, we can rise to the challenge and learn to manage our resources at such a deep level that we can reverse the process and potentially generate an abundance of resources in our lives.

Like Lucky Luciano, a Sicilian-American gangster who rose from being a grubby street urchin, through the ranks of organized crime, to become the director of a crime syndicate. He earned the nickname "Lucky" because he successfully evaded arrest on a number of occasions and eventually became famous for racketeering in narcotics, prostitution, slot machines, loan sharking, and 'protection'. He was indicted and sentenced to thirty to fifty years in prison, but his power continued to grow, even while in jail, as he issued orders and ruled from his cell. Asked near the end of his life if he would do it all again, he replied, *"I'd do it legal. I learned too late that you need just as good a brain to make a crooked million, as an honest million."*[21]

The key here is to realize that our soul's focus is actually on our values, and these are reflected in the resource challenge we face, so with this placement it is good to ask ourselves what we really value in life. As we live up to our values, our self-esteem increases, which is a better way to evaluate our progress than material possessions.

Material restraint is another manifestation of this placement. American novelist Ken Kesey, who was a major counterculture figure in the 1960's with his troupe, the Merry Pranksters, was also a moral critic in his writing. All of his works are about prisoners, some who realize their position and rail against it, others who are just doing their time. His most famous is *One Flew Over the Cuckoo's Nest*, about a petty criminal who's been sentenced to a relatively short prison term but has been transferred to a mental institution. Upon his arrival, he rallies the patients to take on the oppressive head nurse.

This 2nd House placement can also manifest as a physical condition in the body. Swiss psychiatrist Carl Jung developed fainting spells at age twelve, which kept him out of school. As a result, he dreamt for hours, was out in nature, drew, *"but above all...was able to plunge into the world of the mysterious."*[22] When he overheard his father talk of financial concerns around his illness however, he realized he could overcome the fainting spells and was able to return to school.

Or it can manifest as cultural dislocation which forces us to understand the influence of the culture in which we live. The first African American president, Barack Obama, is the child of a Kenyan man and an American woman. His father returned to Africa when he was two, and Barack lived in Hawaii with his mother and grandparents. After she married an Indonesian, she took him with her when she moved to her new husband's native country. Young Barack was then sent back to Hawaii at age ten to live with his grandparents. Thirty-eight years later, when he became the first black American president, it catalyzed a watershed shift of values in American culture which encouraged diversity, inclusivity, and representation.

At the spiritually evolved level this placement can also bring a sublime peace of mind, as we are freed from the shackles of material dependency. This is simply expressed by Indian spiritual master, Sri Meher Baba, who has this placement, in his catchphrase: 'Don't worry, be happy'.

Indian saint and mystic, Krishna, who also had this placement, believed that all religious paths lead to God-consciousness. As a child, when he was overwhelmed by beauty and emotion, he would lose consciousness in ecstatic trances. Later he became "positively insane" and spent several years in a state of "divine madness or inebriation" during which visions of deities appeared to him. Then he met a master of Tantric discipline, who became his first guru and guided him through a remarkable transformation that enabled him to overcome his sense of separation from the world.

Third House

With Sedna in the 3rd House, we are on a spiritual quest to investigate ideas and our everyday communications. Relationships with siblings, neighbors, co-workers, and fellow students will be important and we will want to explore our deepest spiritual needs in our everyday communication. As a result, we will find the stories that our friends and acquaintances tell us of their lives fascinating and will likely sense the spiritual needs behind them.

However, at the unconscious level, we can also have a bit of a blind spot to these needs in ourselves and others and may not recognize them until we are confronted by them in our communication. Unfortunately, we may not understand our needs in that moment and, rather than transcending the experience, we may try to blindly hang on.

As always, our spiritual needs can be subverted by the ego into manipulation of others. Like the famous German playwright and poet, Bertold Brecht, whose operas and plays champion alienation. Despite his intentionally shabby dress, unwashed stench, rotting teeth and icy persona, he was able to hypnotize almost everyone he met into doing his bidding. The saddest case is that of a young German writer from the provinces, Margaret Steffin, who had the misfortune to fall under his spell at an early age. She was almost single-handedly responsible for at least seven major plays, a novel, and countless poems and stories, all of which were published under his name. He was not able to read the source material in French for the works, and the manuscripts are all in her handwriting.

With this placement we might not realize that other people may not be able to relate to these spiritual needs, either in us, or themselves. In fact, sometimes they may even feel threatened by the expression of our spiritual destiny, particularly if that is likely to change the nature of established wisdom.

Or we might realize it and feel daunted by the prospect. Like Charles Darwin, whose theory of evolution has had such a far-reaching impact on human societies across the world, that a "Darwinian Revolution" has been accepted as having taken place. Sensing this potential in his ideas, he hesitated to make his theory widely known in his own lifetime. His wife was religious, and he also seems to have feared for his own and his family's perceived respectability if he challenged the beliefs of the church by making his controversial evolutionary views public.

There can also be health problems, like losing the voice, which occur at key points in our growth, when we are off our spiritual course. These should be seen as signs that we need to look a little deeper at our spiritual needs and make changes in our everyday communications to facilitate them.

With this placement, we will definitely benefit from quiet periods of introspection and should cultivate recreational practices in our lives which assist this, like walking in nature, sitting by the sea, or meditation.

Our broader communications will likely 'stir things up' socially, with the expected full range of possible responses from all sides of society, which will generate new communication crises to assist our ongoing growth.

Betty Friedan was a deeply committed young radical activist, who, when she was laid off for being pregnant, began writing about family and work for women's magazines, saying *"I did it in the morning, like secret drinking"*. She authored the best-seller, *The Feminine Mystique*, which exposed the "desperate housewives" of 1950s America, women imprisoned in suburbia with little to do. Later she helped found the National Organization for Women and served as its first president.

The crisis we encounter in our communication is there to help us grow in consciousness and, as we do, we will likely communicate our growing consciousness and assist this growth in others by taking on a teaching role, writing books, giving lectures, or doing stand-up comedy.

Like German author, Heinrich Boll, who was awarded the Nobel Prize for Literature. Many of his novels and stories describe the personal lives of people struggling to sustain themselves against the wider background of war, terrorism, political divisions, and profound economic and social transition. In a number of them there are protagonists who are stubborn and eccentric individualists opposed to the mechanisms of the state, or of public institutions. His villains are the figures of authority in government, business, the mainstream media, and in the Church, whom he castigates, sometimes humorously, sometimes acidly, for what he perceived as their conformism, lack of courage, self-satisfied attitude, and abuse of power.

And at the spiritual level, legendary French American astrologer, Dane Rudhyar, has this placement. He was heavily influenced in his youth by the radical ideas of Nietzsche, and he had an early mystical experience in which he "became intuitively aware of the cyclic nature of all existence and of the fact that our Western civilization was coming to an autumnal conclusion." He learned astrology at a time when he was also studying the psychological writings of Carl Jung, so he developed an approach that brought astrology and Jungian psychology together. He was one of the first to postulate that the stars do not cause the effects seen in human life, explaining: *"They detail psychological forces working in individuals, but do not override human freedom in responding to those forces"*. He called his new interpretation Humanistic Astrology.

Fourth House

With Sedna in the 4th House, we are on a spiritual quest to investigate our emotional ground, our home environment, our heredity, and our family relationships, both of our birth family and of the family we form as an adult.

With this placement, we live in an evolutionary research laboratory. The karmic influence from the parent of the opposite sex sets up the thrust of this research, which will shape our lives and our influence on the world.

Thomas Edison, the inventor of the light bulb, didn't go to school, but he literally had laboratories in his home, or beside his home from childhood. Author and lecturer, Helen Keller's home was turned into a communication laboratory by an illness that robbed her of her sight and hearing as a young child.

We have likely spent a number of lifetimes exploring the themes that we are researching in our home and enter this life with a deep knowing about these, of which we are seldom conscious and some karmic challenges and likely karmic abilities, which will be illustrated by the aspects to Sedna.

American writer, Emily Dickinson, was shy and fastidious. She had poor health and a reclusive and seemingly uneventful life. She lived together with her domineering father, who was an attorney, and her mother who "did not care for thought", dying in the house where she was born. She was one of three children, with an older brother and a younger sister who were her closest companions. She created a wall of isolation around herself, which she believed was critical to artistic expression. During her lifetime she had seven poems published anonymously, but after her death her sister found a manuscript of almost 900 poems, for which she is now acclaimed to be the greatest female poet of the English language.

Stressful aspects can indicate illness, particularly early in life, which is likely to keep us at home more than usual. However, this illness frequently acts to push our destiny in a particular direction, or to focus our energy. And if the Sedna destiny is embraced, in later life we may well call the illness a 'blessing in disguise'.

Thomas Edison had a hearing problem from an early age, however this didn't stop him inventing the phonograph, the forerunner of our compact disc, or MP3 player. In fact, he credited the phonograph's success to his poor hearing, because it made him push his employees to perfect it so that he could hear it, which meant it was of commercial quality when it hit the market.

The thrust of our evolutionary lifestyle will inevitably collide with everyday lifestyles repeatedly, throughout our life. When we are young this process is largely unconscious, and we may appear to be a victim in these collisions. However, if the Sedna energy is embraced, in later life the reverse effect will occur, and normal lifestyles will be evolutionarily enhanced with each collision.

Oprah Winfrey is an American talk show hostess, actress and business executive, who was born into poverty in rural Mississippi to a teenage single mother. She has stated that she was molested during her childhood and early teens and became pregnant at fourteen. However, she went on to create a more intimate confessional form of media communication, the *Oprah Winfrey Show*, which became the highest-rated television program of its kind in history.

It is possible with this placement that we grew up in a dysfunctional, perhaps even violent, family and that we were the brunt of the negativity. This could have been connected to either our mother, or our father, or our family history. Someone with this placement grew up in a household with a sociopathic mother, who tried to sabotage her. For many years she held on until she lost her father, and that gave her the freedom to let go and "became what she had to be".

Another example is a Welsh television personality, Paula Yates, who was a flirtatious celebrity interviewer. As a child, she had an uncomfortable relationship with her dad, a television star. He was sixteen years-older than her mother, who was a former showgirl, actress, and writer of erotic novels. From age eight, she lived mostly with her mother, and only discovered via DNA testing when she was 38, that the star was not her father at all.

As we grow up, we may feel lost in a sea of emotions and need to escape to find our own sense of belonging. Behavioral traits learned in early childhood, particularly from the parent of the opposite sex, will play a central role in our psyche as we age.

Stressful aspects with Sedna and other 4th House planets and stressful transits to Sedna can indicate forced separation of family members in some way, at some point in our life, leading to a transcendence to a larger spiritual perspective.

Isaac Newton was a British astronomer, physicist, mathematician, and astrologer who showed how the universe is held together. However, he had a difficult childhood. His father died before he was born, and his mother remarried when he was young and left him in the care of his grandparents. Yet he is often described as one of the greatest names in the history of human thought. He was interested in the occult and very likely carried out secret experiments in alchemy, seeking to combine both his scientific and spiritual understanding of the Universe.

If the transition to a larger spiritual perspective is achieved, then the family relationships, particularly with any children, will flower as Sedna moves on to transit the 5th House and the family will become a great source of joy.

Fifth House

With Sedna in the 5th House, we are on a spiritual quest to investigate our passion, our creativity, our self-expression, and the offspring of this, including artwork and children. This is the house of dating, love affairs, and romance and Sedna's placement here can bring deep crises which we must transcend in our love life.

Mata Hari was a Dutch prostitute and exotic dancer who also served as a spy. She was expelled from convent school because she was seduced by a priest, and at the age of eighteen, she moved to Java with her forty-year-old husband. The couple had a violent marriage and when one of their two children died, she left and returned to Europe. There, she used her Javanese dance training to get work in Paris as a nude belly dancer. She also attended German espionage school but was arrested as a double agent during WW1 and executed by firing squad. However, after her death documents revealed that she was simply an elegant but naive adventuress, now known for being the first strip-tease dancer.

At this unconscious level, we can be helpless in the face of these crises in our love affairs, either because we didn't see them coming, or because we are an active participant in them. In the extreme, we might fall prey to someone's predatory behavior or alternatively behave as a predator ourselves.

Like the Italian octogenarian Margherita Pezzoni, who married a twenty-three-year-old when she was ninety-three. Sprightly and lucid of mind, she explained that she wanted to protect him with her estate as she was fond of him. She wanted to adopt him, but it would take too long, so she married him instead. When she died mysteriously two years later, her young husband was left the small inheritance of her pension, not the fortune he anticipated. He was arrested later that year on suspicion of killing another woman and confessed to the murder of both.

However, as we develop our consciousness and our creativity, these romantic crises will provide deep learning experiences that allow us to rise above them and provide fodder for our almost boundless self-expression.

Like D.H. Lawrence, who was a British novelist and poet. He was one of the most controversial writers of the twentieth century, who thought that we should bring our instinct into balance with our intellect. At twenty-six, with two novels in progress, he accepted a luncheon invitation from his favorite teacher and his aristocratic wife. According to legend, she had him in her bed within twenty minutes of meeting him. Two months after that they eloped to Germany, marrying a couple of years later when her divorce became final. His best-known work *Lady Chatterley's Lover* was banned in England and the U.S. for describing sexual intercourse in minute detail.

Or our romantic crises might manifest like those of Red Skelton, who was an American Emmy-award-winning TV comedian. At seventeen he met a fifteen-year-old usherette, and they were married two years later. Soon she was writing his material and managing his career. She negotiated a $1,500-a-week movie contract for him with MGM when he was twenty-five and he went on to appear in over forty movies. CBS then offered him his own variety show, which was an instant success. When it was eventually canceled, he hit the stage and played to sold-out audiences well into his seventies. He had divorced amicably from his first wife at thirty and she continued to manage his career and write for him. He divorced his second wife at sixty and, that same year, he married his third wife, who was twenty-five years his junior. At a frail eighty-four, he continued to write every morning, still happily married to his third wife of the previous twenty-four years.

With this placement, we have a deep need to find out who we are, why we are who we are and why things work as they do, and to bring something into this world as a result of this investigation. This is the root of the creativity of the 5th House.

Many of our well-known astrologers have Sedna in the fifth, including Liz Green, who wrote books like *Saturn: A New Look at an Old Devil,* and founded the Centre for Psychological Astrology in London. And Marc Edmund Jones, who wrote books like the *Guide To Horoscope Interpretation* and, with gifted clairvoyant Elsie Wheeler, created the Sabian Symbols, a set of symbols for every degree of the zodiac. And Jeff Green, whose books include *Pluto: The Evolutionary Journey of the Soul,* and who founded the School of Evolutionary Astrology.

One of the more meaningful ways we can bring something into this world is by having children, so children are therefore another feature of this placement and will likely bring us deep joy. However, we are conscious of the responsibility of parenting and of the sacrifice of our creative time required and so, depending on other factors in the chart, we might also respond to this by having children late in life, or not have them at all. If we do have children however, we will be a very devoted parent.

American actress, Diane Keaton, never married, although she had some substantial romances in her past, notably with Al Pacino, Warren Beatty, and Woody Allen. At the age of fifty she adopted a baby girl, becoming a single mother with her first child. Five years later she adopted a son. She later said of having children, "Motherhood has completely changed me. It's just about the most completely humbling experience that I've ever had."

At heart, with this house placement, we are incurable romantics, and our lives will not prosper if we prioritize practicality over romance. So, we have to learn to follow our heart and express ourselves and, if this lesson is learned early, then our daily rhythm will flower as Sedna moves on to transit the 6th House.

Sixth House

With Sedna in the 6th House, we are on a spiritual quest to investigate the magic that lies underneath each moment of our daily routines and to find a way to service this process and a daily practice to assist with the momentous evolution currently underway.

On a personal level, this placement can also bring comfort in the small pleasures of our daily routine or burden us with never-ending chores. If we are feeling this burden, the key to releasing it is to find meaning in these everyday tasks and thereby turn them into rituals. Once we have found meaning and pleasure in the little jobs, then we are more than capable of handling the bigger ones.

At the unconscious level, however, we may first suffer victimization in our job, or daily routine, and may respond by victimizing and abusing in our turn. Some pressure will catalyze our search for meaning in our work. If we hang on desperately, this pressure becomes victimization, or alienation and breeds more of the same, unless we let go of the old daily routine and transcend to a new one where we can find pleasure and meaning in our work.

If Sedna energy is not dealt with consciously, it is likely to manifest as health issues, particularly early in life, but these can dissipate once we embrace the evolutionary energy of the planet and do the homework of looking after ourselves. With this placement, we will benefit from meditation, prayer, regular exercise, and a healthy diet.

Antonin Artaud was a French dramatist, poet, and theater director, widely recognized as one of the major figures of the European avant-garde. He was plagued by physical and mental hardships throughout his life. He contracted meningitis at age four, which he survived, but was severely weakened. During five years of "rest cures" at a sanatorium he was prescribed laudanum, precipitating a lifelong addiction to that and other opiates. He suffered his first nervous breakdown at age nineteen. His best-known work is the two manifestos of the *Theatre of Cruelty*. There he proposed a theatre that was, in effect, a return to magic and ritual. In true Sedna fashion, he proposed *"a theater in which violent physical images crush and hypnotize the sensibility of the spectator seized by the theatre as by a whirlwind of higher forces."* [23]

Sedna has a deep knowing of which we are seldom conscious and in the 6th House this manifests as an instinctive drive to sort out the bugs in the system. Early in life we will likely do this unconsciously and only become aware of this role through events that force transcendence in our daily work.

James Lovelock, the British independent scientist, and father of Gaia Theory has this placement. As does Ray Kurzweil, the American scientist, inventor, and futurist who predicts a singularity of consciousness in the 2040's through Artificial Intelligence. Each has turned their daily jobs into a unique service to humanity, and both have become prophets of the new evolutionary consciousness that is coming into being with the discovery of Sedna.

As we see, with this placement there is likely to be an evolution in our daily work, which may be forced by hard aspects and encouraged by flows, leading to a transcendence to a larger spiritual perspective.

Joseph Campbell also had Sedna in the 6th House, and he has given us a good view of the spiritual level of the planet. He was an American mythologist, writer, and lecturer, best known for his work in comparative mythology and comparative religion. He was a strong believer in the psychic unity of mankind and its poetic expression through mythology. He believed that the whole of the human race can be seen as engaged in the effort of making the world *"transparent to transcendence"*, by showing that underneath the world of phenomena lies an eternal source which is constantly pouring its energies into this world of time, suffering, and ultimately death.

This eternal source is Sedna and with this planet in the 6th House we have to find our unique way to manifest this source energy in our lives on a day-to-day basis and, through this process, find a way to serve from the perspective of the big spiritual picture. If this lesson is learned early, then our close relationships will flower as the planet moves on to transit the 7th House.

Seventh House

With Sedna in the 7th House, we are on a spiritual quest to investigate our intimate relationships and partnerships, which will provide a rich source of learning experiences tailored perfectly for our growth.

At the unconscious level the normal boundaries on our relationships are not evident to us. So, at the extreme and depending on other factors in the chart, we may have a fascination with abusive relationships, or suffer abuse or victimization ourselves, or become an abuser.

Like Squeaky Fromme, an American woman who attempted the assassination of President Gerald Ford at twenty-six. She was a worshipful follower of ritual cult leader and psychopath, Charles Manson, and wanted to get his message out. She decided to shoot Ford to get the publicity that would put her on TV. She fumbled the attempt, which got her publicity, but she also was sent to prison, and she never did get Manson, or his message across. She was released from jail at the age of sixty.

We have very deep feelings for our partners and may try to control them for our own benefit, or find we are being controlled by them at a very deep level. These deep emotions might overwhelm us at some crisis point, leading us to lash out violently to set it right as we see it, only to come into confrontation with the law as a result. Kidnapping is an extreme form of this control, occasionally found in case studies with this placement, and occurring normally in childhood, with one parent kidnapping a child from the other parent.

The crises we experience in our relationships occur to help us grow in consciousness and our romantic relationships are likely to also bring us these growth opportunities.

Like American sex reformer, Margaret Sanger, who was a prominent advocate for birth control and reproductive rights. She remained a virgin through her first marriage up to the age of thirty-seven. Her first child to her second husband was stillborn and she disowned her second child when he married his true love. However, by the age of seventy-three she had a lover who was thirty-five years younger. This was an unexpected, but significant, connection in her later years that brought her happiness and companionship.

Our business partnerships can also give us some important opportunities to develop our consciousness, though, again, we have to be careful who is in control. Business partners are there to maximize their return and some are prepared to use the full extent of the law or go beyond the law to get an advantage.

Walt Disney lost control of his first successful cartoon character, because he didn't own the rights. By the time he created Mickey Mouse he made sure his business partnerships were solid, but he still had to do the deals required to make it successful, some of which worked, and some didn't. He grew through this and eventually achieved global domination.

At the spiritual level, we can transcend these relationship issues, rising above the give and take in our relationships to accept them as they are and adopt a more care-taking role, rather than one that seeks to gain advantage.

Like American singer, songwriter, Leonard Cohen, who had a small audience for his initial novels and poetry, then had success selling songs to singers and followed this with building a huge audience for his own songs. However, during a period of deep depression in his early forties, he separated from his wife and began to embrace Zen. For a time, he worked in both worlds, the commercial world of music and the spiritual world, until he finally yielded completely and moved to the Zen Centre. Leaving his finely tailored suits for modest robes, and his Hollywood mansions for a small cabin with a narrow cot, he moved up the mountain to cook for the small community, which involved rising at 3am for morning meditation and to begin preparation of the day's menu.

Or, like the founder of modern nursing, Florence Nightingale. She did not think of herself as deeply religious, however, when she was seventeen she felt that God spoke to her, calling her to a future of service. Fearing she would make herself unworthy of this calling, she rejected the frivolous life that her mother and her social set demanded. She thought that women craved sympathy and were not as capable as men, so she preferred the friendship of powerful men, insisting they had done more than women to help her attain her goals. Some scholars believe that she remained chaste for her entire life, perhaps because she felt such a religious calling to her career. Much of her writing, including her extensive work on religion and mysticism, was published after her death.

Eighth House

With Sedna in the 8th House, we are on a path of evolutionary research into the metaphysical world, exploring the connections between people, and between the psychic world and physical reality. This exploration is likely breaking taboos and bringing hidden issues to light.

We might react to this mission by denying it and avoid delving into esoteric matters at all, rejecting God and calling ourselves atheists. With this approach we are also likely to avoid intimacy and will be interacting most of the time on a fairly superficial level.

However, this is the house of life, death, and rebirth. It deals with basic survival issues like sex, money, and intimacy, as they relate to power, control, and the need to manipulate others or be manipulated. So, these themes are going to manifest in our experience one way or another.

Like British-American actor, comedian and bizarre character star, Peter Sellers. He was the only child of variety-show troupers and grew up in theatrical boarding houses. He was close to his overbearing mom, who died when he was forty-two, and he claimed to be able to communicate with her after her death. Though he made more than fifty films, in the industry he had a reputation for being a monster who was hard to work with, impossibly difficult and 'basically not a nice man'. Once during a marital fight, he tried to kill a puppy. He abused his friends, and even wrote his children out of his will, developing into an odd man who became haunted by death and who took drugs to enhance sex.

Another example is American pop singer, Britney Spears, who was a fabulous success by age nineteen. Her trim teenage figure and scant costumes were seen on every magazine cover and yet she attributed her wonderful success to her family and her faith in God. As she grew more famous, however, she became more impulsive. She got married and separated in the same weekend to a childhood friend. She married a second time later that year and, over the next two years, had two children. However, after only two years, she filed for divorce and was often in the news for increasingly bizarre and often self-destructive behavior, till the court revoked her child visitation rights. She bounced back the next year, however, to make a top earning world tour.

The founder of Apple, Steve Jobs, also had this placement. He was called a haunted house by his high school sweetheart who lived with him and was an early Apple employee. She said he became a threatening monster and their relationship fell apart amid wild recriminations when she became pregnant with his first child. He denied he was the father, despite a positive paternity test, and he paid a pittance in child support, while living the life of a millionaire.

Sedna in the 8th House can also indicate compulsions and inherited health issues. Steve had compulsive diet issues, where he would go on fasts and spend weeks eating the same thing - carrot salad with lemon, or just apples - and then suddenly spurn that food and declare that he had stopped eating it. Even at a young age his daughter Lisa began to realize his diet obsessions reflected a life philosophy, one in which asceticism and minimalism could heighten subsequent sensations. *"He believed that great harvests came from arid sources, pleasure from restraint"* she noted. *"He knew the equations that most people didn't know: Things led to their opposites."*[24]

Sedna in the 8th House can also indicate psychic or intuitive contact with the dead and other interdimensional entities.

The father of modern holistic medicine, Edgar Cayce, also has this placement. At the age of 13, he experienced an angelic presence who promised he'd be a healer. He first thought it was his mother, until he ran into her room, and she just sent him back to bed. That day he was in a daze in school, couldn't spell, and was kept after class. That night he slept on his spelling book and remembered every word. Until then he had done poorly in school while afterward, he did well.

The nature of the evolutionary research we undertake will collide with existing reality structures throughout our lives and may raise fears in those who feel threatened by our research, who may attack us in order to defend their world view. When we are young this process is largely unconscious and we may appear to be, or even feel like a victim in these encounters, but later in life such encounters will encourage our evolutionary process.

Solving his own health crisis by putting himself into self-hypnosis, Edgar Cayce started doing readings for others. He doubted the validity of his readings to start with, but he overcame his doubts by observing the amazing accuracy and unfailing benefit of them for healing. He was a devout Christian who read the Bible from beginning to end every year of his life. Yet his readings emphasized the importance of comparative study of belief systems from around the world, the underlying principle of which is the oneness of all life, acceptance of all people, and a compassion and understanding for every major religion.

Through the research into the metaphysical world encouraged by this placement, there is likely to be an evolution in our consciousness, which may be forced by hard aspects and encouraged by flows, leading to a transcendence to a larger spiritual perspective.

Gurumayi is a female Indian guru, who practices Siddha Yoga and has this to say about her philosophy: *"We recognize that in this human life we have a rare opportunity to transform an ordinary perception of this universe, into an extraordinary vision. To be on this planet and to behold the universe from the divine perspective is a sign of an illuminated heart. To put this vision to use in the best way possible is a human being's highest duty."*[25]

If the evolution of consciousness destined by this Sedna placement is achieved, then the philosophies generated by our research will flower as Sedna moves on to transit the 9th House.

Ninth House

With Sedna in the 9th House, we are on a spiritual quest to investigate our beliefs and our search for new horizons. Something hereditary, or an event early in our lives, will likely motivate us on this quest. Or we might remain doggedly at the unconscious level, clinging to our old beliefs, until a confrontation later in life forces us to shift.

The 9th House is about reaching out into the unknown and making sense out of it. However, at an unconscious level, Sedna in the 9th can give us a blindspot to our own ignorance, a sort of blind faith, or spiritual arrogance, where we tune out all information which doesn't support our view. The second in command of the Nazi war machine, Hermann Göring, is an example, he condoned measures leading to mass murder and was eventually hanged.

Or we could be trapped in a blindspot as a child because of the karmic decisions of our parents, like being brought up in religious cult, or being slowly poisoned by them to obtain welfare benefits. Or we may manifest the blindspot simply by not seeing another person, or nor seeing the consequences of how we are treating them, and this lack of respect can enrage people, leading to an attack.

Sedna in the 9th House may indicate tendencies toward narcissistic personality disorder because the social nature and intense focus of the life mission mean the unevolved native can't see past themselves. Donald Trump is a good example of someone with this placement with an unconscious Sedna, which therefore manifests as a blindspot.

Higher education is another feature of the ninth house, so life-changing experiences may occur at school. This can take any form. One person with this placement was a drug addict, with his addiction starting at school. Or we might have life-changing accidents that come from the culture of the school, like a practice of hazing, which can damage us physically as well as psychologically.

We are natural philosophers and, here again, an early alienation can set up a philosophical confrontation later in life.

Ted Kaczynski was an American terrorist, called the Unabomber. As an infant, he was hospitalized for several weeks, and his parents were discouraged from visiting him and prevented from holding him in their rare visits. He was never the same. As an adult, he resigned from a professor's position, moved to a remote shack, and lived on very little. Then he sent several letter bombs, before announcing that he would quit his bombing campaign if a document was published arguing that technological progress was harmful.

With this placement, we might become a learned scholar of law, science, politics, or government policies. Sonia Gandhi, an Italian-born Indian politician, met her husband at university. Her mother-in-law, who was the Indian president, was assassinated and her husband became president. Then he was assassinated, and she went into retreat, while she transcended the experience, then stood for election herself.

As we develop our consciousness, Sedna in the 9th House encourages us to explore new horizons. Like French author and feminist, Simone de Beauvoir, who challenged social traditions with her writing. She started by publishing her ideas on love at twenty-two, then went on to run an avant garde salon and edit a publication called the *Nouvelle Revue*.

Richard Branson, a British entrepreneur with this placement, wrote in his autobiography about his decision to start an airline: *"My interest in life comes from setting myself huge, apparently unachievable challenges and trying to rise above them ... from the perspective of wanting to live life to the full, I felt that I had to attempt it."*

At the spiritually evolved level, this placement can bring profound spiritual, or religious understanding.

Like American theosophist, esoteric astrologer and author, Alice Bailey, who was unhappy in her youth and broke away from her early environment at twenty-two to become an evangelist and social worker. Then at 41, she transcended and founded an occult school which explored the nature of the soul, the hierarchical structure of the universe, and principles of spiritual evolution. Her teachings on unity, global cooperation, and the integration of science and spirituality, align with many principles of the New Age movement, a term she coined, including the focus on personal spiritual growth, holistic healing, and consciousness transformation.

Tenth House

With Sedna in the 10th House, we are on a spiritual quest motivated by our place in society, or events in our professional lives, which will likely be played out in public view. Depending on our level of consciousness, we might be totally unaware of this mission, or we might actively seek an evolutionary social caretaker role. Either way, our developing consciousness will entail job, or career changes, which may involve crises so severe that we must transcend them to reach a new level of consciousness.

At the unconscious level, this may manifest through acts of arrogance, rebellion, betrayal, or victimization, in which we might be playing either the victim, or the perpetrator role. With this placement, we inherently feel the oneness of humanity, but at this level we may not understand that others don't see this, which might lead us to adopt a deluded social mission.

Like Rudolf Hess, the deputy leader of the Nazi party, who believed that he was obeying supernatural powers and had a mission to end the war, when he flew from Germany to Scotland, taking it on his own to attempt negotiations with England. Unfortunately, this was a delusion and Hitler denied his authority, calling him insane. He was imprisoned and spent the next forty-one years in Spandau prison, and for the last twenty-one years he was the sole inmate.

The development of our consciousness may involve periods where we feel isolated, or alienated within the social context of our lives, while we absorb lessons and build up steam to re-engage in a new way. However, as we grow in consciousness, we will likely become prominent in our chosen field, because of our integrity, our problem-solving skills and our insights. As a result, society will likely hold us in high regard for these skills.

As we develop spiritually, our conviction about the oneness of humanity, may inspire us to take visionary leadership.

Like German philosopher, Arthur Schopenhauer, who thought the phenomenal world was the product of 'a blind and insatiable metaphysical will'. He believed that will is a fundamental metaphysical power that blindly and incessantly drives the world and is at the root of human suffering and dissatisfaction. He led a solitary life, deeply involved in the study of Buddhist and Hindu philosophies. While he was a misogynist who never marrying and discouraged friendships, his writing on aesthetics, morality, and psychology, exerted an important influence on the world, and he has had an important posthumous impact.

With Sedna in the 10th House, we are likely to evolve through changes in our career, which may be forced by hard aspects and encouraged by flows, leading to a transcendence to a larger spiritual perspective.

The first American woman in space, and first known LGBT astronaut, Sally Ride, was asked, 'Was it spiritual as you kissed the heavens?" She responded, *"You know, what was absolutely amazing to me was the feeling I had looking* back at earth . . . how beautiful our planet is, and how fragile it looks." She then convinced NASA to set up a Mission to Planet Earth, to use space technology to understand how both man-made and natural shifts are affecting our environment.

At the spiritual level, we will likely publicly live our beliefs, like the couple who opened their home to refugees during World War Two, at great risk to their family. He had Sedna in the tenth and she in the second. They were both made saints, the first time a husband and wife have both been honored in this way.

Or like Dutch Indonesian spiritual leader, Pakh Subuh, who founded a new form of Islamic mysticism in which the supplicant is initiated by means of a kind of 'meditative communal submission to divine understanding', a method of communion that involves surrender.

At this level, our sense of the oneness of humanity can inspire us to take visionary leadership. Like the Dalai Lama, who is the spiritual leader of the Tibetan people. He was born on a straw mat in a cowshed to a farmer's family in a remote part of Tibet and yet by the time he was eighty, he had become one of the most popular world leaders. This recognition came despite great personal difficulty. He was enthroned during a war with China and forced to sign an agreement to incorporate Tibet into China. Then, fearing for his life in the wake of a revolt nine years later, he fled to India, from where he led a government in exile.

Or our visionary leadership might be like that of Albert Einstein, the scientist whose Theory of Relativity laid the groundwork for 20th century physics and provided the essential structure of the cosmos. Experiencing the universe as a harmonious whole, he encouraged the use of intuition to solve problems, marveled at the mystery of God in nature and applauded the ideals of great spiritual teachers such as Buddha and Jesus. *"I like to experience the universe as one harmonious whole. Every cell has life. Matter, too, has life; it is energy solidified. Our bodies are like prisons, and I look forward to be free, but I don't speculate on what will happen to me. I live here now, and my responsibility is in this world now. I deal with natural laws. This is my work here on earth."*[26]

Eleventh House

With Sedna in the 11th House, we are on a spiritual mission to explore social ideals and the collective consciousness, and we will likely immerse ourselves in groups of like-minded people and, over time, build a group of loyal friends to help us on our mission.

At the unconscious level, however, we might feel a little lost at sea in the popular culture of society, which at this stage of mankind's development is still often fairly primitive and violent. So, there is a danger of abuse which is simply accepted by our group as normal and so unspoken or is a hidden side effect of our social group. Or we could take on an abusive mission ourselves.

With this placement we are likely to work with organizations and groups that promote our personal values. We are focused on goals for the future and, because of the ideals we come to represent, we may become idolized by large numbers of people, but we may also attract vilification and victimization.

We may be born with innate ideals, which will then be conditioned by our early years and will drive our lives. If the birth environment is not conducive to our innate ideals, we can experience situations where we feel victimized from an early age and these feelings will then shape our beliefs and the ongoing collisions will either reinforce this or cause us at some point to reject the early ideology and replace it with something more appropriate.

Osama bin Laden was born into a wealthy family. His mother was his father's tenth wife, but she was Syrian and was called the slave by the rest of the family. Osama was called the son of the slave. This early sense of victimization was formative in shaping his perspective. He projected this onto his fellow Muslims and set out to save them from, as he saw it, the decadent Saudi Arabian leadership who were in alliance with the infidels.

If the birth environment is conducive to our innate ideals, our first collision with social norms will probably come at school when our personality is already well formed, and we are less likely to feel victimized by the challenge.

Clockwork Orange is a dystopian novel set-in a near future English society featuring a subculture of extreme youth violence. The teenage protagonist narrates his violent exploits and his experiences with state authorities who are intent on reforming him. Author, Anthony Burgess, who has this placement, called it 'a play of the spirit', as it was written in just three weeks.

Either way, our ideals will be tested in the forge of the community and later in life, if strengthened through experience, they are likely to collide with the prevailing norms of the social environment in a way that helps us evolve. These ongoing collisions then serve to advance our evolutionary mission, and, through this work, there is likely to be an evolution in consciousness leading to a transcendence to a larger spiritual perspective.

Jules Verne was a French writer widely popular for his science fiction novels and amazing anticipation of future discoveries. Regarded as the father of science fiction, he predicted the use of submarines, helicopters, air conditioning, guided missiles, trips to outer space and motion pictures long before they were developed. Though he was raised Catholic, he became a deist from his early forties. Deism is a philosophical position that posits that a god does not interfere directly with the world. It also rejects revelation as a source of religious knowledge and asserts that reason and observation of the natural world are sufficient to determine the existence of a single creator of the universe.

Shivabalayogi was a meditation guru who attained self-realization through twelve years meditating in a state of total thoughtlessness for an average of twenty hours a day. For the next three decades, he traveled extensively in India and Sri Lanka, initiating over ten million people into meditation. Then he traveled for four years in England and the United States doing the same. His teaching emphasized the need for spiritual practice to achieve self-realization.

If the evolution in consciousness promised by this placement is achieved, then the ideals embraced by this mission will flower as Sedna moves on to transit the 12th House.

Twelfth House

With Sedna in the 12th House, we are on a spiritual quest to transcend the collective dreams and ambitions of the popular culture in which we find ourselves immersed and rediscover the deep connection with life and appreciation of the universe that we inherently feel inside.

With this placement, forces outside of our control will shape our lives in crucial ways and we may be placed in a caring role, or a self-caring role, early in life, so we grow up deeply caring and able to respond appropriately to situations that may overwhelm other people.

Like Louis Armstrong, who was an American jazz trumpeter, known for his sense of humor and vivid energy. He grew up poor among prostitutes and street-people in New Orleans, singing on the street corners in the Old Quarter to help his family. Later he became a world-class eccentric, his own man, brash and irreverent, with a top-ten hit in every decade for half a century and well known for his classic, *What a Wonderful World*.

We likely have a deep empathy for people as a result and understand that we are each on our own mission, each with a story to tell and challenges to face. This is the house of subconscious realms, of work behind the scenes, and of institutions.

At this unconscious level our mission may be more reflective of the collective dreams and ambitions that we sense around us and there is a danger of falling victim to the desire to con people by not revealing ourselves, or to manipulate the collective through the stories we tell.

Or we may try to lose ourselves in the crowd with this placement, but then we become a creature of the crowd and open ourselves to abuse by the system. Or we might engage in abusive behavior in an attempt to influence the system.

An extreme example is Charles Manson, a ritual cult leader, and psychopath who had a band of drug-numbed followers. He was the illegitimate son of a teenage prostitute and an army colonel, and he was raised by an aunt and uncle. Unable to keep his friendships, and unsuccessful with his music, he began to prophesy chaos, then directed a series of ritual grisly killings in a deluded attempt to start a race war.

Or conversely, we might become an exemplar for people, like the first man to set foot on the moon, Neil Armstrong, who has Sedna right on the twelfth house cusp. He famously said as he took that step: 'One small step for a man! One giant leap for mankind!' This statement exemplifies our potential with Sedna in the twelfth house.

Or we could inspire the collective, like Carl Sagan, who, as a child, is said to have gazed with awe at the heavens and speculated on the existence of life beyond earth. He became a noted authority on planetary atmospheres and surfaces and his book *Cosmos* was a bestseller. The TV series by the same name was seen by more than 500 million people in sixty countries and he inspired a generation with his enthusiastic lectures, books and documentaries about space and life.

The greatest potential for self-mastery, expression of genius and true profession comes out of this house, but only after the karma of self-imprisonment and bondage to our unconscious motivations has surfaced and been resolved. So, it is important with this placement that we learn to judge our own needs and choose when to help others, and when to switch off and nurture ourselves. Recreational activities which mix exercise and contemplation, like hiking or sailing, can be beneficial.

As we grow, we likely become conscious of the karma we are carrying which needs resolution in this lifetime, and also of the new dharmic seeds we are sowing for future life work. Through this process, there is likely to be an evolution in our consciousness, which may be forced by hard aspects and encouraged by flows, leading to a transcendence to a larger spiritual perspective.

Sedna in the twelfth can indicate a personal interface with the spiritual world, consciously or otherwise. This is the house of past life experiences and we have likely spent a number of lifetimes exploring spiritual themes, so we enter this life with a deep love and appreciation of the universe.

Irwyn Greif has been a practicing American psychic from the age of twenty-five, specializing in reincarnation readings. He has written a number of books, notably *The Soul Is a Traveler in Time*, describing his psychic experiences and angel contacts. His book is designed to help raise consciousness levels and give readers an understanding of what lies beyond our five senses, beyond our earthly plane, and even beyond our comprehension.

At some point in our soul development, we will have to integrate our individuated concept of ourselves with the cosmic, social, and natural elements surrounding us. This concept of 'self in society' will be tested in the forge of life and is likely, later in life, to challenge the prevailing norms in an evolutionary way.

Like German writer, teacher and philosopher, Immanuel Kant, who was the foremost thinker of the Enlightenment and considered one of the greatest philosophers of all time. He was a short man, scarcely five feet tall, and he had a deformed chest. He suffered from poor health throughout his life, and because of this, he maintained a strict regimen of walking. However his systematic and comprehensive work on ethics and aesthetics inaugurated a new era in the development of philosophical thought, particularly in the various schools of Idealism. He lectured on many subjects including logic, metaphysics, and moral philosophy. His style was humorous and vivid, and he used many examples from his wide reading to enliven his subjects. Though often charged with attacking metaphysics, he believed in the existence of God and in a future life and is often described as an ethical Rationalist.

Appendix 1

Discover Where the Dwarf Planets Are for You

This appendix will assist you in discovering in which house each of the dwarf planets are placed in your birth chart. The houses are the different areas of our lives, like relationships or occupation, in which the planetary energies play out. The key information you need is: the date, the time, and the place of your birth.

You need your birth time to work out the houses. If you don't know the time of your birth, read through all the house interpretations, and see which you relate to most. If you have an approximate birth time, calculate your chart based on that time, and read the interpretation for your house placement, as well as the ones on either side.

To find out in which houses your new planets are placed:

a. Go to www.astro.com and either create a free account, or click "Create a horoscope immediately as a guest user".

b. Input your birth data on the Birth Data Entry screen and click "Continue".

c. Then choose "Extended Chart Selection" on the next screen or find this option under "Charts & Data" in your account.

d. On this data screen, at the bottom left under "Additional Objects", you choose the dwarf planets, which are listed as Asteroids, by highlighting them.

The dwarfs in this box are *Eris, Haumea, Ixion, Makemake, Orcus, Quaoar, Sedna, and Varuna.*

e. Then opposite this, in the box on the bottom right, add the numbers **225088, 120347** to also include *Gonggong & Salacia.*

f. If you want to see the aspects – angles of relationship - between your dwarf planets and the traditional planets, click the box beside "to all objects" under the heading, "Aspects", under "Display and calculation settings". (This book doesn't cover aspects, so only do this if you understand them already).

g. Click "Show the Chart" to see it. Symbols, or glyphs, are used for the traditional planets, which may be confusing if you are new to the language of astrology. However the dwarf planets are identified on the chart using the first five letters of their name, making it easy to locate them.

h. The houses are the 12 segments of the circle numbered 1 to 12 where they converge at the centre. See Appendix 2 for more details on the Houses.

i. Write down your house placement for each of the 10 dwarf planets or print your chart out so you can reference the house position of each planet as you read this book.

Appendix 2
Astrology Basics

If you are brand new to astrology, welcome! Let's quickly demystify the birth chart and explain the basics of astrology, so we're all on the same page. As you look at your chart, imagine you are born at the center point, and everything in the top semi-circle was in the sky above you when you were born. All the planets in the bottom semi-circle were on the other side of the planet.

Radiating out from the center you'll see there are 12 numbered segments of the circle. These pie slices are the astrological houses, which are the different areas of our lives in which the planetary energies play out. The ones in the bottom semi-circle are the 6 personal houses, and those in the top semi-circle are the 6 social houses.

The 1st House is about who we are inside - our identity, our ego stepping forth into the world as an individual. The 2nd House is about the physical reality in which we find ourselves - our resources, possessions, and income, as well as our self-esteem. The 3rd House is about the ideas and communication that occurs in our physical reality - about our writing, speaking, teaching, and research.

The 4th House is about our home - our sacred ground, where we feel rooted. The 5th House is about the things we do in our home - the love affairs we have and the children or artwork that we create. And the 6th House is our daily routine - our health, and the services we provide, or jobs we do.

Moving into the top semi-circle, the 7th House is about our one-to-one relationships – how we meet another, and the deals we make in those relationships. The 8th House is about our joint resources and, at a deeper level, about the hidden energies - the spirit world and the occult magic that underlies everything. The 9th House is about the understanding that comes through that deep exploration - and through activities like travel and education.

The 10th House is our social life and profession – our place in the world. The 11th House is about the people we meet socially – the groups we engage in and our participation in the collective consciousness. And the 12th House is the house of spirituality - of the collective unconscious or the zeitgeist within which we live.

There is a polarity relationship between the personal and social houses which stand opposite each other. For example, the 1st House is about the self and the 7th House is our relationships to others. The 2nd House is our personal resources and the 8th House is about joint resources. The 3rd House is about ideas and communication and the 9th House is about the knowledge that those ideas and communications bring us.

All of the houses are functioning in our chart, whether we have planets in them or not. The houses that do have planets are emphasized, however, as that is the area of our lives in which the planet's energy will play out.

Now let's consider the planets. The planets from the Sun out to Saturn are called the inner planets and they each represent a different aspect of our personality. Those beyond Saturn are called the outer planets, and they each represent a different aspect of our consciousness.

The **Sun** is the center of our solar system and represents our will to live. It talks about our ego and our pride, and our self-realization as a unique being. It provides the energy for all the other parts of our personality. We connect strongly with the Sun's placement in our charts, which explains the popularity of Sun Sign astrology.

The **Moon** is our feeling center, talking about our comfort zone and our subconscious world. It infuses the past into our lives through our feelings. Our emotions are instinctive survival reactions that we have learned from an early age. They help us mediate each moment and deal with events in our lives. So, the Moon is responsive, receptive, and reflective, encouraging us to be spontaneous and instinctual in our reactions.

Mercury is the winged messenger of the gods, and he talks about our ideas and communication. He is inquisitive and curious, and he encourages us to write and talk. He loves to organize, and he can make us adaptable and versatile, but also highly-strung, nervous, indecisive, and overly technical.

Venus is the planet of values. We tend to think of her as ruling relationships but that is because, when we value someone, we draw them to us. So, she talks of love and romance, but also of money, beauty, and art. She's all about the pleasure we take in life, our artistic inclinations, and what makes us happy.

Mars is the assertive male principle, and he talks about our agency in the world. He gives us drive, fueling our ambition and enabling us to assert ourselves. Mars is also the sexual component of our relationships. Our Mars enables us to be assertive, directed, forthright, and adventurous. But also perhaps impulsive, rash, impatient, aggressive, and forceful.

Next, we have our new inner dwarf planet, **Ceres**. She talks of nurturing and of the give and take of love required in each day to survive. She gives us a love of the simple, natural, wholesome, and unadorned. She encourages unconditional love, and talks about the relationships between parents and children, and all the issues of devotion, attachment, separation, sacrifice, loss, and grief.

Then we have **Jupiter**, who is tolerant and speaks to us of belief and grace. He is the planet of expansion, of being more than we are. We do this through travel, through education, and through the lucky breaks we get simply by being in the right place at the right time. So he talks about our good fortune and the successes we achieve, but also about our generosity and gratitude, and the hope and honor that comes as a result.

Which brings us to the traditional outer limit of the solar system, **Saturn**, the planet of responsibility. Saturn is the teacher, bringing us the hard lessons that we have to learn as well as the material rewards which come from living up to those demands. So, he talks about maturity, responsibility, and discipline, and he encourages us to be patient, stable, reliable, persevering, and diligent.

The relationships between the planets in the chart are called aspects and they talk about how the planets involved function together. We don't use them in this book, however. And we normally think of the Star Signs, Aries, Taurus, etc, as being essential in astrology, but they talk of collective influences, and so we don't use them either.

One other technique to familiarize yourself with is that of higher octaves, where outer planets are considered higher octaves of inner planets. The inner planets talk of aspects of personality and are familiar to us. Because the outer planets represent aspects of consciousness, we can understand them is as a more spiritual expression of an inner planet energy.

Appendix 3
Dwarf Planets as Higher Octaves

Higher octaves offer us a framework to help us understand the dwarf planets. A higher octave expresses an inner planet energy at a more spiritual level. (The dwarf planets are listed in bold).

Sedna – Ceres – Moon

Makemake – Uranus – Mercury

Haumea – Neptune – Venus

Eris – Pluto – Mars

Quaoar – Jupiter

Varuna – Saturn

We can think of **Sedna** as the higher octave of **Ceres**, who is our newly reclassified inner dwarf planet. Ceres is our ability to love and be loved. At both a basic level and in the bigger sense of the word, she represents what we need to feed and nourish ourselves. And we can think of Ceres as the higher octave of the Moon. The Moon is our emotional center, mediating our survival moment to moment, and Ceres mediates our survival over time. Sedna steps this heart-centered energy all the way out to the new limit of our solar system, so she talks of our survival over lifetimes.

We can look at **Makemake** as the higher octave of Uranus, which is traditionally the higher octave of Mercury. Makemake gives Uranus's intuitive impulses meaning and context, which transforms our understanding of his unexpected ways. And Uranus's lateral web gives Mercury's detail an energetic network to organize and connect his information. All three planets are tricksters, and Makemake is a spiritual trickster who allows us to experiment with the area of life signified by his position in our chart.

We can think of **Haumea** as the higher octave of Neptune, where Neptune's psychic opening has the potential to blossom into real psychic connection with Haumea, a connection to the soul level. Neptune is traditionally considered to be the higher octave of Venus, echoing her values and aesthetics at a higher spiritual level. We see a love of beauty and a belief in values in all three of these bodies.

In mythology **Eris** is the warrior sister of Mars, and in our lives, where Mars is fighting mundane battles, Eris' challenge is on a more esoteric level. In modern astrology **Pluto** is considered to be the higher octave of Mars, so we can look at Eris as the higher octave of Pluto. She steps up his transformative energy to a fierce grace through which everything in our lives is opened to the light and can be transmuted into love.

We can look at **Quaoar** as the higher octave of Jupiter. Both planets talk of expansion and of new possibilities, but where Jupiter expands through a mix of luck and a hunger for more, Quaoar repolarizes Jupiter so we can see the new opportunities and deftly take the appropriate action to enable the expansion that is possible in each moment. Where Jupiter is a sort of dumb luck, Quaoar turns each moment into a dynamic meditation, where we can see the opportunities and act on them in real time. So, Quaoar is like smart luck.

And we can think of **Varuna** as the higher octave of Saturn. Both are supreme rulers, but where Saturn limits, controls, and structures, Varuna transmutes this energy into self-sufficient mastery. However, like Saturn, Varuna can place restrictions on us if we are not being true to ourselves or honest with others, but these dissipate when we forgive and align with Spirit.

Gonggong – Salacia – Mars/Venus

I look at **Gonggong** as being the higher octave of **Salacia**, who I see as the higher octave of Venus and Mars combined. Venus/Mars is all about relationship and sexuality, and Salacia steps that up to a psychic level, while Gonggong steps that up even further to an empathic contact.

Ixion – Pluto – Orcus

Pluto also has two new brothers who share his orbit as well as his angle to the ecliptic. All three are at the same octave level. The two brothers are, however, polar opposites. The first is the seeker consciousness of **Ixion**, who enables us to develop our authenticity. The second, **Orcus**, opens us to karmic consciousness. He teaches us to align with a spiritual creed and understand the karmic process of life.

And we have to remember the higher octaves act on the lower octaves to repolarize and transform them, as Dane Rudhyar reminds us in the below quote from Horoscope Magazine.

When Uranus, Neptune and Pluto are considered as "higher" expressions of such planets as Mercury, Venus and Mars... the closer planets are seen to represent a "lower octave" of biological-personal functions or energies; the more remote ones, beyond Saturn, a "higher octave" constituted of more transcendent and "spiritual" activities or qualities of being.

There is some truth, no doubt, in such statements if one restricts oneself to a consideration of only the external events of a person's life. The "illuminations" which Uranus may bring to the consciousness that is not frozen into Saturnian rigidity can inspire and transform the Mercury mind. The compassion and inclusiveness which are characteristic of Neptune do act directly — if allowed by Saturn so to act—upon the sense of value and the feeling-judgments represented by Venus. The power of inescapable destiny and total surrender to a cause, which defines essentially Pluto's operations, do transform — if allowed to do so — the strictly personal initiative of Mars.

But the essential fact is that the activities of Uranus, Neptune and Pluto run counter to the normal functions of Mercury, Venus and Mars. The former are not just personal activities of a "higher" kind; they are activities meant to disturb and transform — indeed, utterly to repolarize and reorient those of Mercury, Venus and Mars.[27]

Appendix 4
Dwarf Planet University

The information in this book comes out of collective research at the Dwarf Planet University, where we are pioneering the astrological exploration of the Kuiper Belt. The dwarf planets speak of new aspects of consciousness that are arising in our lives, and to support on-boarding each of them, we offer 6 week courses to explore the planets in our birth chart and the charts of the other class members. We embody each aspect of consciousness simply by studying the house placement, the aspects and then researching the transits. All within a supportive environment.

The course format mixes webinars, blog-posted assignments, and live Zoom Q&A's, so you can attend from anywhere in the world. We start with a live Welcome Q&A and we explore the house position in the first fortnight, the aspects in the second, and the transits in the third. Each fortnight includes an instructional webinar, an investigative assignment based on your personal chart and a live 2 hour Zoom Q&A session.

Assignments are posted on a private forum so we can learn from, and comment on, posts from our fellow course members. And the live Q&A sessions are recorded so we can pick up classes we miss.

The students on our courses range from absolute beginners to very experienced astrologers, and this range is the source of the vibrant class culture. Students love the community sharing that occurs through the blog-posted assignments and the live Zoom Q&As. Through this sharing we gain a good picture of how these new planets act similarly, and yet diversely, in each of our lives.

We offer a Dwarf Planet Astrology Diploma on completion of any 8 of our 10 courses, but you are also welcome to do courses singly and in any order. All the courses have a mix of ongoing and casual students, which provides a creative cross pollination of experience levels.

What Students Say:

I highly recommend the Dwarf Planets Course for the insights and the amount of new information and perspective gathered. Alan's teaching inspires one and brings new light and spiritual understanding to charts (certainly to mine). His humor and friendly approach made the seminars very enjoyable, yet profound.

Elisabetta Quintiliani, Italy

Alan Clay's sensitive, cutting edge wisdom and the community sharing make the classes on the Dwarf Planets compelling and profound. They are as much an exploration as a revelation. Not only mentally stimulating, they are a deep dive into each of our psyche and growth experience. I love them and am looking forward to more.

Karen La Puma, Astrologer, Counsellor, Speaker

I'm very grateful for Alan Clay's insightfully powerful dwarf planet courses. He offers a supportive and welcoming class environment that encourages learning and processing the deep new consciousness of these planets. I totally recommend engaging with this outer realm of alchemy into our inner self!

Sue Rose Minahan, Evolutionary Post-Modern Astrologer

What Alan Clay has created with the Dwarf Planet University is nothing short of genius. His in-depth knowledge and amazing teaching style are unique and what the astrological world has been waiting for. I'm so enjoying learning about our far-reaching dwarf planets amongst a galaxy of friendly, intelligent student astrologers from all over the universe, logging on at their differing time zones.

Eileen Richardson, UK.

Alan Clay's work has transformed my thinking—about my chart, about my practice—even about astrology itself. Alan is a born teacher.

Ariel Harper Nave, Canada

I absolutely loved the class! As a first time student of astrology, I can honestly say that aside from Alan (a wonderful teacher and guide), every one of the students in the class was a teacher for me. I learned so much and can't wait for the next class to begin.

Mary Anne Pitt, USA

Who would have thought that studying the dwarf planets would lead to such an expansive awareness of my soul's journey? For this, I am very grateful. The style and structure of Alan's teaching provides the group with a very warm, safe and informative space in which to learn. I love being part of the group. Thank you, Alan.

Marian Ryan, Energy Therapist, Author, Teacher, UK

As one returning to astrological study after decades away, I find Alan's instruction fun and informative, and the classroom format a gift of shared learning for everyone participating. Alan has created a safe and supportive space where anyone, at any level of knowledge, can thrive and shine. His obvious love of this work illuminates its presentation. I echo the comments of others, "Best astrology classes ever!"

Nalini MacNab, USA

"I have been sensing a reciprocity in my study of the dwarf planets. As I shift focus and embrace each of their unique energies, I am in turn rewarded by a richer understanding of myself and the world in which we live."

Alison Glennie, Ireland

Appendix 5
Meet the Writer

New Zealander, Alan Clay, is a transpersonal astrologer, who specializes in the outer planets. Inspired by the work of Dane Rudhyar, Alan's work has broadened over the years into a study of the new dwarf planets, and today he is one of the Kuiper Belt's astrological pioneers.

For many years, Alan worked internationally as a clown and a clown teacher. He describes clown as being "a big research into people and what makes us human". And he combined this research with astrological consulting to explore the depths and potentials of the human psyche.

Alan's well-known clown textbook, *Angels Can Fly,* includes a mix of clown theory, workshop and street exercises, anecdotes from 20 international clowns, and fictional stories that follow the adventures of 10 street clowns.

He is also the writer and director of an award-winning romantic comedy film, *Courting Chaos,* in which a Beverly Hills girl falls for a Venice Beach street clown called Chaos, and she must overcome her inhibitions and become a clown herself for the relationship to survive.

His novel, *Believers in Love,* tells the story of a father and daughter team of sand-sculptors, who embark on a crazy adventure from Bondi Beach to a magic mountain in New

Zealand, exploring the transient nature of art and life, to discover that dreams are real. Reviewers called it *"A book about love, laughter and life. Not just a story, this is an exploration of emotion and philosophy. A novel of journey and self-discovery."*

Alan's first astrology book, *Sedna Consciousness, the Soul's Path of Destiny* was launched at the United Astrology Conference 2018 in Chicago. It is the ultimate reference on Sedna, the new outer limit of our solar system, and includes aspect interpretations with all the traditional planets, as well as the new dwarf planets.

Following several years of teaching dwarf planet astrology courses online, Alan founded the Dwarf Planet University under the Jupiter/Saturn conjunction in 2020. Since then he has developed all the course material that is used by students at the Uni, and he leads the fortnightly live Zoom Q&A's. He still works as a consulting astrologer and is available for chart readings by Zoom.

In 2023 the Dwarf Planet University started publishing a series of textbooks on the new planets. *The Astrology of Haumea, Neptune's Higher Octave* was released in May and *The Astrology of Makemake, Uranus' Higher Octave* in October. These books are co-written by Alan and his assistant, Melissa Billington.

Endnotes

1. https://www.theguardian.com/books/2016/apr/20/groucho-marx-the-comedy-of-existence-lee-siegel-review-biography
2. https://jcf.org/about-joseph-campbell/follow-your-bliss/
3. https://www.lofficielusa.com/music/lorde-talks-baring-it-all-for-solar-power-album-cover
4. https://highprofiles.info/interview/annie-lennox/
5. https://premierchristian.news/en/news/article/susan-boyle-you-have-to-wait-for-miracles#
6. https://en.wikipedia.org/wiki/Andrew_Cuomo#Controversies
7. https://en.wikipedia.org/wiki/Rosa_Parks#
8. https://en.wikipedia.org/wiki/Betty_Friedan
9. https://www.artspace.com/magazine/interviews_features/in-their-words/the-philosophy-of-jeff-koons-52916
10. https://www.rollingstone.com/music/music-news/van-morrison-to-revisit-moondance-with-reissue-72914/
11. https://www.janegoodall.org.nz/africa-programmes/research/
12. https://www.innerviews.org/inner/bjork.html
13. https://en.wikipedia.org/wiki/Billy_Connolly
14. https://en.wikipedia.org/wiki/Frida_Kahlo
15. https://www.jkrishnamurti.org/about-dissolution-speech#:~:text=I%20want%20to%20do%20a,new%20theories%20and%20new%20philosophies.
16. https://www.azquotes.com/quote/654802
17. Lowe, Janet (January 22, 2001). Oprah Winfrey Speaks: Insights from the World's Most Influential Voice. John Wiley & Sons. p. 122. ISBN 978-0-471-39994-0.
18. Forrest, Steven (2012). Yesterday's Sky: Astrology and Reincarnation. Borrego Springs, CA: Seven Paws Press. pp. 24, 25, 340. ISBN 978-0-9790677-3-0.
19. https://www.smh.com.au/national/keeper-of-secrets-20100521-w230.html
20. George, Demetra, & Bloch, Douglas (2003). Asteroid Goddesses: The Mythology, Psychology, and Astrology. Nicolas-Hays, Inc. ISBN 9780892540822

21 https://www.austinchronicle.com/feedback/2011-10-14/1265857/
22 https://carljungdepthpsychologysite.blog/2020/07/09/carl-jungs-school-years/
23 https://asia-archive.si.edu/essays/article-gillitt/
24 https://lisabrennanjobs.net/writing/confessions-of-lapsed-vegetarian
25 https://www.siddhayoga.org/gurumayi-chidvilasananda
26 https://www.azquotes.com/quote/823417
27 https://www.khaldea.com/rudhyar/astroarticles/planetaryoctaves.php

www.ingramcontent.com/pod-product-compliance
Lightning Source LLC
Chambersburg PA
CBHW041732300426
44116CB00018B/2955